Oxford Introductions to Language Study

MARTINHO

Language and Culture

Claire Kramsch is Professor of
German and Foreign Language
Acquisition at the University of
California at Berkeley.

D0827058

Published in this series:

Rod Ellis: *Second Language Acquisition*
Thomas Scovel: *Psycholinguistics*
Bernard Spolsky: *Sociolinguistics*
H. G. Widdowson: *Linguistics*
George Yule: *Pragmatics*

For Myris

Oxford Introductions to Language Study

Series Editor H.G.Widdowson

Language and Culture

Claire Kramsch

OXFORD UNIVERSITY PRESS

OXFORD
UNIVERSITY PRESS

Great Clarendon Street, Oxford OX2 6DP

Oxford University Press is a department of the University of Oxford.
It furthers the University's objective of excellence in research, scholarship,
and education by publishing worldwide in

Oxford New York

Auckland Bangkok Buenos Aires Cape Town Chennai
Dar es Salaam Delhi Hong Kong Istanbul Karachi Kolkata
Kuala Lumpur Madrid Melbourne Mexico City Mumbai
Nairobi São Paulo Shanghai Taipei Tokyo Toronto

OXFORD and OXFORD ENGLISH are registered trade marks of
Oxford University Press in the UK and in certain other countries

ISBN 0 19 437214 6

Typeset by Tradespools Limited, Frome, Somerset

Printed in China

Contents

Preface

Purpose

What justification might there be for a series of introductions to language study? After all, linguistics is already well served with introductory texts: expositions and explanations which are comprehensive, authoritative, and excellent in their way. Generally speaking, however, their way is the essentially academic one of providing a detailed initiation into the discipline of linguistics, and they tend to be lengthy and technical: appropriately so, given their purpose. But they can be quite daunting to the novice. There is also a need for a more general and gradual introduction to language: transitional texts which will ease people into an understanding of complex ideas. This series of introductions is designed to serve this need.

Their purpose, therefore, is not to supplant but to support the more academically oriented introductions to linguistics: to prepare the conceptual ground. They are based on the belief that it is an advantage to have a broad map of the terrain sketched out before one considers its more specific features on a smaller scale, a general context in reference to which the detail makes sense. It is sometimes the case that students are introduced to detail without it being made clear what it is a detail *of*. Clearly, a general understanding of ideas is not sufficient: there needs to be closer scrutiny. But equally, close scrutiny can be myopic and meaningless unless it is related to the larger view. Indeed it can be said that the precondition of more particular enquiry is an awareness of what, in general, the particulars are about. This series is designed to provide this large-scale view of different areas of language study. As such it can serve as preliminary to (and precondition for) the more specific and specialized enquiry which students of linguistics are required to undertake.

But the series is not only intended to be helpful to such students. There are many people who take an interest in language without being academically engaged in linguistics *per se*. Such people may recognize the importance of understanding language for their own lines of enquiry, or for their own practical purposes, or quite simply for making them aware of something which figures so centrally in their everyday lives. If linguistics has revealing and relevant things to say about language, this should presumably not be a privileged revelation, but one accessible to people other than linguists. These books have been so designed as to accommodate these broader interests too: they are meant to be introductions to language more generally as well as to linguistics as a discipline.

Design

The books in the series are all cut to the same basic pattern. There are four parts: Survey, Readings, References, and Glossary.

Survey

This is a summary overview of the main features of the area of language study concerned: its scope and principles of enquiry, its basic concerns and key concepts. These are expressed and explained in ways which are intended to make them as accessible as possible to people who have no prior knowledge or expertise in the subject. The Survey is written to be readable and is uncluttered by the customary scholarly references. In this sense, it is simple. But it is not simplistic. Lack of specialist expertise does not imply an inability to understand or evaluate ideas. Ignorance means lack of knowledge, not lack of intelligence. The Survey, therefore, is meant to be challenging. It draws a map of the subject area in such a way as to stimulate thought and to invite a critical participation in the exploration of ideas. This kind of conceptual cartography has its dangers of course: the selection of what is significant, and the manner of its representation, will not be to the liking of everybody, particularly not, perhaps, to some of those inside the discipline. But these surveys are written in the belief that there must be an alternative to a technical account on the one hand and an idiot's guide on the other if linguistics is to be made relevant to people in the wider world.

Readings

Some people will be content to read, and perhaps re-read, the summary Survey. Others will want to pursue the subject and so will use the Survey as the preliminary for more detailed study. The Readings provide the necessary transition. For here the reader is presented with texts extracted from the specialist literature. The purpose of these Readings is quite different from the Survey. It is to get readers to focus on the specifics of what is said, and how it is said, in these source texts. Questions are provided to further this purpose: they are designed to direct attention to points in each text, how they compare across texts, and how they deal with the issues discussed in the Survey. The idea is to give readers an initial familiarity with the more specialist idiom of the linguistics literature, where the issues might not be so readily accessible, and to encourage them into close critical reading.

References

One way of moving into more detailed study is through the Readings. Another is through the annotated References in the third section of each book. Here there is a selection of works (books and articles) for further reading. Accompanying comments indicate how these deal in more detail with the issues discussed in the different chapters of the Survey.

Glossary

Certain terms in the Survey appear in bold. These are terms used in a special or technical sense in the discipline. Their meanings are made clear in the discussion, but they are also explained in the Glossary at the end of each book. The Glossary is cross-referenced to the Survey, and therefore serves at the same time as an index. This enables readers to locate the term and what it signifies in the more general discussion, thereby, in effect, using the Survey as a summary work of reference.

Use

The series has been designed so as to be flexible in use. Each title is separate and self-contained, with only the basic format in common. The four sections of the format, as described here, can be drawn upon and combined in different ways, as required by the needs, or interests, of different readers. Some may be content with the Survey and the Glossary and may not want to follow up the suggested References. Some may not wish to venture into the Readings. Again, the Survey might be considered as appropriate preliminary reading for a course in applied linguistics or teacher education, and the Readings more appropriate for seminar discussion during the course. In short, the notion of an introduction will mean different things to different people, but in all cases the concern is to provide access to specialist knowledge and stimulate an awareness of its significance. This series as a whole has been designed to provide this access and promote this awareness in respect to different areas of language study.

H. G. WIDDOWSON

Author's acknowledgments

My understanding of the complex relationship of language and culture has been deepened by the graduate students in applied linguistics at UC Berkeley Graduate School of Education, and by innumerable researchers and language teachers around the world. I am particularly grateful to Linda von Hoene, Eva Lam, Margaret Perrow, Steve Thorne, Greta Vollmer, who read drafts of this book, and to Pete Farruggio and Soraya Sablo who provided some of the data in the Survey. I wish to thank the staff of Oxford University Press for their patient and efficient support. This book would not have come to pass without the encouraging guidance of Henry Widdowson, to whom go my deepest gratitude and admiration. He has helped me bring into focus the very personal view that I present here on language and culture in language study.

This book is dedicated to my first grandson, born at the confluence of seven languages and cultures.

CLAIRE KRAMSCH

Survey

1
The relationship of language and culture

Language is the principal means whereby we conduct our social lives. When it is used in contexts of communication, it is bound up with culture in multiple and complex ways.

To begin with, the words people utter refer to common experience. They express facts, ideas or events that are communicable because they refer to a stock of knowledge about the world that other people share. Words also reflect their authors' attitudes and beliefs, their point of view, that are also those of others. In both cases, *language expresses cultural reality*.

But members of a community or social group do not only express experience; they also create experience through language. They give meaning to it through the medium they choose to communicate with one another, for example, speaking on the telephone or face-to-face, writing a letter or sending an e-mail message, reading the newspaper or interpreting a graph or a chart. The way in which people use the spoken, written, or visual medium itself creates meanings that are understandable to the group they belong to, for example, through a speaker's tone of voice, accent, conversational style, gestures and facial expressions. Through all its verbal and non-verbal aspects, *language embodies cultural reality*.

Finally, language is a system of **signs** that is seen as having itself a cultural value. Speakers identify themselves and others through their use of language; they view their language as a symbol of their social identity. The prohibition of its use is often perceived by its speakers as a rejection of their social group and their culture. Thus we can say that *language symbolizes cultural reality*.

We shall be dealing with these three aspects of language and culture throughout this book. But first we need to clarify what we mean by culture. We might do this by considering the following poem by Emily Dickinson.

Essential Oils – are wrung –
The Attar from the Rose
Be not expressed by Suns – alone –
It is the gift of Screws –

The General Rose – decay –
But this – in Lady's Drawer
Make Summer – When the Lady lie
In Ceaseless Rosemary –

Nature, culture, language

One way of thinking about culture is to contrast it with nature. Nature refers to what is born and grows organically (from the Latin *nascere*: to be born); **culture** refers to what has been grown and groomed (from the Latin *colere*: to cultivate). The word culture evokes the traditional nature/nurture debate: Are human beings mainly what nature determines them to be from birth or what culture enables them to become through socialization and schooling?

Emily Dickinson's poem expresses well, albeit in a stylized way, the relationship of nature, culture, and language. A rose in a flower bed, says the poem, a generic rose ('The General Rose'), is a phenomenon of nature. Beautiful, yes, but faceless and nameless among others of the same species. Perishable. Forgettable. Nature alone cannot reveal nor preserve the particular beauty of a particular rose at a chosen moment in time. Powerless to prevent the biological 'decay' and the ultimate death of roses and of ladies, nature can only make summer when the season is right. Culture, by contrast, is not bound by biological time. Like nature, it is a 'gift', but of a different kind. Through a sophisticated techno-logical procedure, developed especially to extract the essence of roses, culture forces nature to reveal its 'essential' potentialities. The word 'Screws' suggests that this process is not without labor. By crushing the petals, a great deal of the rose must be lost in order to get at its essence. The technology of the screws constrains the exuberance of nature, in the same manner as the **technology of the word**, or printed syntax and vocabulary, selects among the many potential meanings that a rose might have, only those that best express its innermost truth—and leaves all others unsaid. Culture makes the rose petals into a rare perfume, purchased at high cost, for the particular, personal use of a particular lady. The lady may die, but the fragrance of the rose's essence (the Attar) can make her immortal, in the same manner as the language of the poem immortalizes both the rose and the lady, and brings both back to life in the imagination of its readers. Indeed, 'this' very poem, left for future readers in the poet's drawer, can 'Make Summer' for readers even after the poet's death. The word and the technology of the word have immortalized nature.

The poem itself bears testimony that nature and culture both need each other. The poem wouldn't have been written if there were no natural roses; but it would not be understood if it didn't share with its readers some common assumptions and expectations about rose gardens, technological achievements, historic associations regarding ladies, roses, and perfumes, common memories of summers past, a shared longing for immortality, a similar familiarity with the printed word, and with the vernacular and poetic uses of the English language. Like the screws of the rose press, these common collective expectations can be liberating, as they endow a universal rose with a particular meaning by imposing a structure, so to speak, on nature. But they can also be constraining. Particular meanings are adopted by the **speech community** and imposed in turn on its members, who find it then difficult, if not impossible, to say or feel anything original about roses. For example, once a bouquet of roses has become codified as a society's way of expressing love, it becomes controversial, if not risky, for lovers to express their own particular love without resorting to the symbols that their society imposes upon them, and to offer each other as a sign of love, say, chrysanthemums instead—which in Germany, for example, are reserved for the dead! Both oral cultures and literate cultures have their own ways of emancipating and constraining their members. We shall return to the differences between oral and literate cultures in subsequent chapters.

The screws that language and culture impose on nature

correspond to various forms of **socialization** or **acculturation**. Etiquette, expressions of politeness, social *dos* and *don't*s shape people's behavior through child rearing, behavioral upbringing, schooling, professional training. The use of written language is also shaped and socialized through culture. Not only what it is proper to write to whom in what circumstances, but also which text genres are appropriate (the application form, the business letter, the political pamphlet), because they are sanctioned by cultural conventions. These ways with language, or norms of interaction and interpretation, form part of the invisible ritual imposed by culture on language users. This is culture's way of bringing order and predictability into people's use of language.

Communities of language users

Social conventions, norms of social appropriateness, are the product of communities of language users. As in the Dickinson poem, poets and readers, florists and lovers, horticulturists, rose press manufacturers, perfume makers and users, create meanings through their words and actions. Culture both liberates people from oblivion, anonymity, and the randomness of nature, and constrains them by imposing on them a structure and principles of selection. This double effect of culture on the individual—both liberating and constraining—plays itself out on the social, the historical and the metaphorical planes. Let us examine each of these planes in turn.

People who identify themselves as members of a social group (family, neighborhood, professional or ethnic affiliation, nation) acquire common ways of viewing the world through their interactions with other members of the same group. These views are reinforced through institutions like the family, the school, the workplace, the church, the government, and other sites of socialization throughout their lives. Common attitudes, beliefs, and values are reflected in the way members of the group use language—for example, what they choose to say or not to say and how they say it. Thus, in addition to the notion of **speech community** composed of people who use the same linguistic code, we can speak of **discourse communities** to refer to the common ways in which members of a social group use language to meet their social needs. Not only the grammatical, lexical, and phonological features of their language (for example, teenage talk, professional jargon, political rhetoric) differentiate them from others, but also the topics they choose to talk about, the way they present information, the style with which they interact, in other words, their **discourse accent**. For instance, Americans have been socialized into responding 'Thank you' to any compliment, as if they were acknowledging a friendly gift: 'I like your sweater!'—'Oh, thank you!' The French, who tend to perceive such a compliment as an intrusion into their privacy, would rather downplay the compliment and minimize its value: 'Oh really? It's already quite old!' The reactions of both groups are based on the differing values given to compliments in both cultures, and on the differing degrees of embarrassment caused by personal comments. This is a view of culture that focuses on the ways of thinking, behaving, and valuing currently shared by members of the same discourse community.

But there is another way of viewing culture—one which takes a more historical perspective. For the cultural ways which can be identified at any one time have evolved and become solidified over time, which is why they are so often taken for natural behavior. They have sedimented in the memories of group members who have experienced them firsthand or merely heard about them, and who have passed them on in speech and writing from one generation to the next. For example, Emily Dickinson's allusion to life after death is grounded in the hope that future generations of readers will be able to understand and appreciate the social value of rose perfume and the funeral custom of surrounding the dead with fragrant rosemary. The culture of everyday practices draws on the culture of shared history and traditions. People identify themselves as members of a society to the extent that they can have a place in that society's history and that they can identify with the way it remembers its past, turns its attention to the present, and anticipates its future. Culture consists of precisely that historical dimension in a group's identity. This diachronic view of culture focuses on the way in which a social group represents itself and others through its material productions over time—its technological achievements, its monuments, its works of art, its popular culture—that punctuate the development of its historical identity. This material culture is reproduced and preserved through institutional mechanisms that are also part of the culture, like museums, schools, public libraries, governments, corporations, and the media. The Eiffel Tower or the Mona Lisa exist as material artifacts, but they have been kept alive and given the prominence they have on the cultural market through what artists, art collectors, poets, novelists, travel agents, tourist guides have said and written about them. Language is not a culture-free code, distinct from the way people think and behave, but, rather, it plays a major role in the perpetuation of culture, particularly in its printed form.

Imagined communities

These two layers of culture combined, the social (synchronic) and the historical (diachronic), have often been called the **sociocultural context** of language study. There is, in addition, a third essential layer to culture, namely, the imagination. Discourse communities are characterized not only by facts and artifacts, but by common dreams, fulfilled and unfulfilled imaginings. These imaginings are mediated through the language, that over the life of the community reflects, shapes, and is a metaphor for its cultural reality. Thus the city of London is inseparable, in the cultural imagination of its citizens, from Shakespeare and Dickens. The Lincoln Memorial Building in Washington has been given extra meaning through the words 'I have a dream ...' that Martin Luther King Jr. spoke there in 1963. Rose gardens have been immortalized in the French imagination by Ronsard's poetry. Language is intimately linked not only to the culture that is and the culture that was, but also to the culture of the imagination that governs people's decisions and actions far more than we may think.

Insiders/outsiders

To identify themselves as members of a community, people have to define themselves jointly as insiders against others, whom they thereby define as outsiders. Culture, as a process that both includes and excludes, always entails the exercise of power and control. The rose press in the Dickinson poem, one could argue, yields exquisite perfume, but at a high price. Not only must the stem and the petals be ultimately discarded, but only the rich and powerful can afford to buy the perfume. Similarly, only the powerful decide whose values and beliefs will be deemed worth adopting by the group, which historical events are worth commemorating, which future is worth imagining. Cultures, and especially national cultures, resonate with the voices of the powerful, and are filled with the silences of the powerless. Both words and their silences contribute to shaping one's own and others' culture. For example, Edward Said describes how the French constructed for themselves a view of the culture of 'the Orient' that came directly from such writers as Chateaubriand, Nerval, and Flaubert, and that only served, he says, to reinforce the sense of superiority of the European culture. The Orient itself was not given a voice. Such **orientalism**, Said argues, has had a wide-ranging effect on the way Europeans and Americans have viewed the Middle East, and imposed that view on Middle Easterners themselves, who implicitly acquiesce to it when they see themselves the way the West sees them. Similarly, scholars in Gender Studies, Ethnic Studies, Gay Studies, have shown the **hegemonic** effects of dominant cultures and the authority they have in representing and in speaking for the Other. Ultimately, taking culture seriously means questioning the very base of one's own intellectual inquiry, and accepting the fact that knowledge itself is colored by the social and historical context in which it is acquired and disseminated. In this respect, language study is an eminently cultural activity.

As the considerations above suggest, the study of language has always had to deal with the difficult issue of **representation** and representativity when talking about another culture. Who is entitled to speak for whom, to represent whom through spoken and written language? Who has the authority to select what is representative of a given culture: the outsider who observes and studies that culture, or the insider who lives and experiences it? According to what and whose criteria can a cultural feature be called representative of that culture?

In the social, the historic, and the imagined dimension, culture is heterogeneous. Members of the same discourse community all have different biographies and life experiences, they may differ in age, gender, or ethnicity, they may have different political opinions. Moreover, cultures change over time as we can see from the difficulty many contemporary readers might have with the Dickinson poem. And certainly Ladies in the nineteenth century imagined the world differently from readers at the end of the twentieth. Cultures are not only heterogeneous and constantly changing, but they are the sites of struggle for power and recognition, as we shall see in Chapter 7.

In summary, culture can be defined as membership in a discourse community that shares a common social space and history, and common imaginings. Even when they have left that community, its members may retain, wherever they are, a common system of standards for perceiving, believing, evaluating, and acting. These standards are what is generally called their 'culture'.

The Emily Dickinson poem has served to illuminate several aspects of culture:

1 Culture is always the result of human intervention in the biological processes of nature.

2 Culture both liberates and constrains. It liberates by investing the randomness of nature with meaning, order, and rationality and by providing safeguards against chaos; it constrains by imposing a structure on nature and by limiting the range of possible meanings created by the individual.

3 Culture is the product of socially and historically situated discourse communities, that are to a large extent imagined communities, created and shaped by language.

4 A community's language and its material achievements represent a social patrimony and a symbolic capital that serve to perpetuate relationships of power and domination; they distinguish insiders from outsiders.

5 But because cultures are fundamentally heterogeneous and changing, they are a constant site of struggle for recognition and legitimation.

The different ways of looking at culture and its relationship to language raise a fundamental question: to what extent are the world views and mental activities of members of a social group shaped by, or dependent on, the language they use? The theory that languages do affect the thought processes of their users has been called the theory of **linguistic relativity**.

Linguistic relativity

Philologists and linguists have been interested in the diversity of human languages and their meanings since the eighteenth century. The discovery by European scholars of oriental languages like Sanskrit, or the ability to decipher the Egyptian hieroglyphs at the end of the eighteenth century, coincided with a revival of nationalism in such countries as France and Germany, and was accompanied by increased interest in the unique cultural characteristics of their national languages. The romantic notion of the indissociability of language and culture promoted by German scholars like Johann Herder (1744–1803) and Wilhelm von Humboldt (1762–1835), in part in reaction to the French political and military hegemony of the time, gave great importance to the diversity of the world's languages and cultures. These scholars put forward the idea that different people speak differently because they think differently, and that they think differently because their language offers them different ways of expressing the world around them (hence the notion of linguistic relativity). This notion was picked up again in the United States by the linguist Franz Boas (1858–1942), and subsequently by Edward Sapir (1884–1939) and his pupil Benjamin Lee Whorf (1897–1941), in their studies of American Indian languages. Whorf's views on the interdependence of language and thought have become known under the name of **Sapir–Whorf hypothesis**.

The Sapir–Whorf hypothesis

The Sapir–Whorf hypothesis makes the claim that the structure of the language one habitually uses influences the manner in which one thinks and behaves. Whorf recounts an anecdote that has become famous. While he was working as a fire insurance risk assessor, he noticed that the way people behaved toward things was often dangerously correlated to the way these things were called. For example, the sight of the sign 'EMPTY' on empty gasoline drums would prompt passersby to toss cigarette butts into these drums, not realizing that the remaining gasoline fumes would be likely to cause an explosion. In this case, the English sign 'EMPTY' evoked a neutral space, free of danger. Whorf concluded that the reason why different languages can lead people to different actions is because language filters their perception and the way they categorize experience.

So, for example, according to Whorf, whereas English speakers conceive of time as a linear, objective sequence of events encoded in a system of past, present, and future tenses (for example, 'He ran' or 'He will run'), or a discrete number of days as encoded in cardinal numerals (for example, ten days), the Hopi conceive of it as intensity and duration in the analysis and reporting of experience (for example, *wari* = 'He ran' or statement of fact, *warikni* = 'He ran' or statement of fact from memory). Similarly 'They stayed ten days' becomes in Hopi 'They stayed until the eleventh day' or 'They left after the tenth day'.

Whorf insists that the English language binds English speakers to a Newtonian view of objectified time, neatly bounded and classifiable, ideal for record-keeping, time-saving, clock-punching, that cuts up reality into 'afters' and 'untils', but is incapable of expressing time as a cyclic, unitary whole. By contrast, the Hopi language does not regard time as measurable length, but as a relation between two events in lateness, a kind of 'eventing' referred to in an objective way (as duration) and in a subjective way (as intensity). 'Nothing is suggested about time [in Hopi] except the perpetual "getting later" of it' writes Whorf. Thus it would be very difficult, Whorf argues, for an English and a Hopi physicist to understand each other's thinking, given the major differences between their languages. Despite the general translatability from one language to another, there will always be an incommensurable residue of untranslatable culture associated with the linguistic structures of any given language.

The Sapir–Whorf hypothesis has been subject to fierce controversy since it was first formulated by Whorf in 1940. Because it indirectly made the universal validity of scientific discoveries contingent upon the language in which they are expressed, it encountered the immediate scorn of the scientific community. The positivistic climate of the time rejected any intimation that language determined thought rather than the other way around; the proposition that we are prisoners of our language seemed unacceptable. And indeed it would be absurd to suggest that Hopis cannot have access to modern scientific thought because their language doesn't allow them to, or that they can gain a sense of Newtonian time only by learning English. One can see how a strong version of Whorf's relativity principle could easily lead to prejudice and racism. After all, it is always possible to translate across languages, and if this were not so, Whorf could never have revealed how the Hopis think. The link between a linguistic structure and a given cultural world view must, it was argued, be viewed as arbitrary.

Fifty years later, with the rise of the social sciences, interest in the linguistic relativity principle has revived. The translatability argument that was levelled against the incommensurability of cultures is not as convincing as it seemed. If speakers of different languages do not understand one another, it is not because their languages cannot be mutually translated into one another— which they obviously can, to a certain extent. It is because they don't share the same way of viewing and interpreting events; they don't agree on the meaning and the value of the concepts underlying the words. In short, they don't cut up reality or categorize experience in the same manner. Understanding across languages does not depend on structural equivalences but on common conceptual systems, born from the larger context of our experience.

The strong version of Whorf's hypothesis, therefore, that posits that language determines the way we think, cannot be taken seriously, but a weak version, supported by the findings that there are cultural differences in the semantic associations evoked by seemingly common concepts, is generally accepted nowadays. The way a given language encodes experience semantically makes aspects of that experience not exclusively accessible, but just more salient for the users of that language.

For example, Navajo children speak a language that encodes differently through different verbs the action of 'picking up a round object' like a ball and 'picking up a long, thin, flexible object' like a rope. When presented with a blue rope, a yellow rope, and a blue stick, and asked to choose which object goes best with the blue rope, most monolingual Navajo children chose the yellow rope, thus associating the objects on the basis of their physical form, whereas monolingual English-speaking children almost always chose the blue stick, associating the objects on the basis of their color, although, of course, both groups of children are perfectly able to distinguish both colors and shapes.

This experiment is viewed as supporting the weak version of the Whorf hypothesis that language users tend to sort out and distinguish experiences differently according to the semantic categories provided by their respective codes. But it also shows that the resources provided by the linguistic code are understandable only against the larger pragmatic context of people's experience. A Navajo child learning English might start categorizing experience in Navajo the way English speakers do. Thus, the generic semantic meanings of the code that have established themselves over time within a given discourse community are subject to the various and variable uses made of them in social contexts. We are, then, not prisoners of the cultural meanings offered to us by our language, but can enrich them in our pragmatic interactions with other language users.

Summary

The theory of linguistic relativity does not claim that linguistic structure constrains what people *can* think or perceive, only that it tends to influence what they routinely *do* think. In this regard, the work of Sapir and Whorf has led to two important insights:

1 There is nowadays a recognition that language, as code, reflects cultural preoccupations and constrains the way people think.

2 More than in Whorf's days, however, we recognize how important context is in complementing the meanings encoded in the language.

The first insight relates to culture as semantically encoded in the language itself; the second concerns culture as expressed through the actual use of the language.

2

Meaning as sign

Language can mean in two fundamental ways, both of which are intimately linked to culture: through what it says or what it refers to as an **encoded sign** (**semantics**), and through what it does as an action in context (**pragmatics**). We consider in this chapter how language means as an encoded sign.

The linguistic sign

The crucial feature that distinguishes humans from animals is humans' capacity to create **signs** that mediate between them and their environment. Every meaning-making practice makes use of two elements: a signifier and a signified. Thus, for example, the sound /rouz/ or the four letters of the word 'rose' are signifiers for a concept related to an object in the real world with a thorny stem and many petals. The signifier (sound or word) in itself is not a sign unless someone recognizes it as such and relates it to a signified (concept); for example, for someone who doesn't know English, the sound /rouz/ signifies nothing because it is not a sign, but only a meaningless sound. A sign is therefore neither the word itself nor the object it refers to but the relation between the two.

There is nothing necessary about the relation between a given word as linguistic signifier and a signified object. The word 'rose' can be related to flowers of various shapes, consistencies, colors, and smells, it can also refer to a color, or to a smell. Conversely, the object 'rose' can be given meaning by a variety of signifiers: Morning Glory, Madame Meillon, flower, *die Rose*, *une rose*. Because there is nothing inherent in the nature of a rose that makes the four letters of its English signifier more plausible than, say, the five letters of the Greek word ῥόδον, the linguistic sign has been called **arbitrary**. Furthermore, because there is no one-to-one correspondence, no perfect fit between signifier and signified, the dualism of the linguistic sign has been called **asymmetrical**.

The meaning of signs

What is the nature of the relation between signifier and signified? In other words, how do signs mean? When Emily Dickinson uses in her poem words like 'rose', or 'rosemary', these words point to (are the **referents** of) objects that grow in the real gardens of the real world. They refer to a definable reality. Their meaning, that can be looked up in the dictionary, is **denotative**. On the other hand, the meaning of 'rose' and 'rosemary' is more than just the plants they refer to. It is linked to the many associations they evoke in the minds of their readers: a rose might be associated with love, passion, beauty; rosemary might be associated with the fragrance of summer and the preservation of dried herbs. Both words draw their meaning from their **connotations**.

In addition to denotation and connotation, there is a third kind of meaning that words can entertain with their objects. For, as with all signifiers, they not only point to, and are associated with, their objects, they can also be images (or **icons**) of them. So, for example, exclamations like 'Whoops!', 'Wow!', 'Whack!' don't so much refer to emotions or actions as they imitate them (onomatopoeia). Their meaning is therefore **iconic**. The Dickinson poem makes full use of iconic meanings. For example, the sound link between the /s/ of 'screw', 'summer', and 'ceaseless rosemary' creates a world of sound signs that replicates the crushing sound of a rose press, thus enhancing iconically the denotative and the connotative meanings of the individual words. In addition, by transforming the 'rose' into the word 'rosemary', the poem offers an icon of the metamorphosis it is talking about with regard to roses. As we can see in this poem, any linguistic sign may entertain multiple relations to its object, that may be simultaneously of a denotative, connotative, or iconic kind.

Cultural encodings

All three types of signs correspond to ways in which members of a given discourse community encode their experience. In that regard, the **code** is not something that can be separated from its meanings.

Different signs denote reality by cutting it up in different ways, as Whorf would say. For example, *table*, *Tisch*, *mesa* denote the same object by reference to a piece of furniture, but whereas the English sign 'table' denotes all tables, Polish encodes dining tables as *stol*, coffee tables or telephone tables as *stolik*. British English encodes anything south of the diaphragm as 'stomach', whereas in American English a 'stomachache' denotes something different from a 'bellyache'. Similarly, Bavarian German encodes the whole leg from the hip to the toes through one sign, *das Bein*, so that '*Mein Bein tut weh*' might mean 'My foot hurts', whereas English needs at least three words 'hip', 'leg', or 'foot'. Cultural encodings can also change over time in the same language. For example, German that used to encode a state of happiness as *glücklich*, now encodes deep happiness as *glücklich*, superficial happiness as *happy*, pronounced /hepi/.

The encoding of experience differs also in the nature of the cultural associations evoked by different linguistic signs. For example, although the words 'soul' or 'mind' are usually seen as the English equivalents of the Russian word *dusha*, each of these signs is differently associated with their respective objects. For a Russian, not only is *dusha* used more frequently than 'soul' or 'mind' in English, but through its associations with religion, goodness, and the mystical essence of things it connotes quite a different concept than the English. Studies of the **semantic networks** of bilingual speakers makes these associations particularly visible. For example, bilingual speakers of English and Spanish have been shown to activate different associations within one of their languages and across their two languages. In English they would associate 'house' with 'window', and 'boy' with 'girl', but in Spanish they may associate *casa* with *madre*, and *muchacho* with *hombre*. But even within the same **speech community**, signs might have different semantic values for people from different **discourse communities**. Anglophone readers of Emily

Dickinson's poem who happen not be members of her special discourse community, might not know the denotational meaning of the word 'Attar', nor associate 'rosemary' with the dead. Nor might the iconic aspects of the poem be evident to them. Even though they may be native speakers of English, their **cultural literacy** is different from that of Emily Dickinson's intended readers (see Chapter 5).

Words can also serve as culturally informed icons for the concepts, objects, or persons they signify. For example, English speakers who belong to certain discourse communities may intensify denotative meanings by iconically elongating the vowel of a word, for example, 'It's beau::::::tiful!'. In French, intensification of the sound is often done not through elongation of the vowel but through rapid reiteration of the same form: *'Vite vite vite vite vite! Dépêchez-vous!'* (Quick! Hurry up!). These different prosodic encodings form distinct ways of speaking that are often viewed as typically English or French. Similarly, onomatopoeia links objects and sounds in seemingly inevitable ways for members of a given culture. For example, the English sounds 'bash', 'mash', 'smash', 'crash', 'dash', 'lash', 'clash', 'trash', 'splash', 'flash' are for English speakers icons for sudden, violent movements or actions. A speaker of another language might not hear in the sound /æʃ/ any such icon at all; for a French speaker the words *hache, tache, crache, sache, cache, vache* have no semantic relationship despite similar final sounds. A French-educated speaker of French might, however, be inclined to hear in words like *siffler* and *serpent* icons of their objects because of the initial similar sounding /s/, but also, as we see below, because of the cultural association with a prior text—the famous line from Racine's *Andromaque*: *'Pour qui sont ces serpents qui sifflent sur nos têtes?'* ('But what are these serpents hissing above our heads?').

It is important to mention that the differences noted above among the different languages are not only differences in the code itself, but in the semantic meanings attributed to these different encodings by language-using communities. It is these meanings that make the linguistic sign into a cultural sign.

Semantic cohesion

We have seen how signs relate words to the world in ways that are generally denotative of common cultural objects, or particularly connotative of other objects or concepts associated with them, or simply iconic. But, as a sign, a word also relates to other words or signs that give it a particular value in the verbal text itself or **co-text**. Beyond individual nouns and sounds, words refer to other words by a variety of **cohesive devices** that hold a text like the Dickinson poem together: pronouns ('it'), demonstratives ('this'), repetition of the same words from one sentence to the next (for example, 'The Attar from the Rose ... The general Rose ... In ceaseless Rosemary') or same sounds from one line to the next (for example, the sound /l/ in 'Lady's Drawer', 'the Lady lie'), recurrence of words that relate to the same idea (for example, 'Suns', 'summer'; 'essential Oils', 'Attar'), conjunctions (for example, 'but', 'when'). These devices capitalize on the associative meanings or shared connotations of a particular community of competent readers who readily recognize the referent of the pronoun 'it' and the lexical reiteration of 'suns' and 'summer', whereas a community of less competent readers might not. Semantic cohesion depends on a discourse community's communal associations across the lines of a poem, or across stretches of talk.

A sign or word may also relate to the other words and instances of text and talk that have accumulated in a community's memory over time, or **prior text**. Thus, to return, for example, to the Russian sign *dusha*, which roughly denotes 'a person's inner core', it connotes goodness and truth because it is linked to other utterances spoken and heard in daily life, to literary quotes (for example, 'His soul overflowing with rapture, he yearned for freedom, space, openness' written by Dostoevsky), or to other verbal concepts such as pricelessness, human will, inner speech, knowledge, feelings, thoughts, religion, that themselves have a variety of connotations. When English speakers translate the word *dusha* by the word 'soul', they are in fact linking it to other English words, i.e. 'disembodied spirit', 'immortal self', 'emotions', that approximate but don't quite match the semantic **cohesion** established for *dusha* in the Russian culture. The meanings of words cannot be separated from other words with which they have come to be associated in the discourse community's semantic pool.

Another linguistic environment within which ,words carry cultural semantic meaning consists of the linguistic **metaphors** that have accumulated over time in a community's store of semantic knowledge. Thus, for example, the English word 'argument' is often encountered in the vicinity of words like 'to defend' (as in 'Your claims are indefensible'), 'to shoot down' (as in 'He shot down all of my arguments'), 'on target' (as in 'Her criticisms were right on target'), which has led George Lakoff and Mark Johnson to identify one of the key metaphors of the English language: 'Argument is War'. Some of these metaphors are inscribed in the very structure of the English code, for example, the metaphor of the visual field as container. This metaphor delineates what is inside it, outside it, comes into it, as in 'The ship is *coming into* view', 'I have him *in* sight', 'He's *out of* sight now'. Each language has its own metaphors, that provide semantic cohesion within its boundaries.

In all these examples, the semantic meanings of the code reflect the way in which the speech community views itself and the world, i.e. its culture. They are intimately linked to the group's experiences, feelings and thoughts. They are the non-arbitrary expression of their desire to understand and act upon their world.

The non-arbitrary nature of signs

We said at the beginning that signs have no natural connection with the outside world and are therefore arbitrary. It is precisely this arbitrariness that makes them so amenable to appropriation by members of culturally embedded discourse communities. Speakers and writers use those signs that are most readily available in their environment, without generally putting them into question, or being aware, as Sapir noted, that other signifying relations might be available. As we noted in Chapter 1, socialization into a given discourse community includes making its signifying practices seem totally natural. Native users of a language, for example, do not view the linguistic sign as arbitrary; on the contrary, they view it as a necessity of nature. Jakobson reports the anecdote of one Swiss-German peasant woman who asked why the French used *fromage* for *Käse* (cheese): *'Käse ist doch viel natürlicher!'* (*'Käse* is so much more natural!'), she added. Only detached researchers and non-native speakers see the relations between signs as mere contingence.

Native speakers do not feel in their body that words are arbitrary signs. For them, words are part of the natural, physical fabric of their lives. Seen from the perspective of the user, words and thoughts are one. For example, anyone brought up in a French household will swear that there is a certain natural masculinity about the sun (*le* soleil) and femininity about the moon (*la* lune). For English speakers, it is perfectly natural to speak of 'shooting down someone's argument'; they don't even think one could talk of arguments in a different way. Having once recognized the semantic cohesion of the Emily Dickinson poem, readers may even come to view the interpretation offered in Chapter 1 as the only one possible—the natural one. Even though, as we have seen, signs are created, not given, and combine with other signs to form cultural patterns of meaning, for native speakers linguistic signs are the non-arbitrary, natural reality they stand for.

The major reason for this naturalization of culturally created signs is their motivated nature. Linguistic signs do not signify in a social vacuum. Sign-making and sign-interpreting practices are motivated by the need and desire of language users to influence people, act upon them or even only to make sense of the world around them. With the desire to communicate a certain meaning to others comes also the desire to be listened to, to be taken seriously, to be believed, and to influence in turn other peoples' beliefs and actions. The linguistic sign is therefore a motivated sign.

Symbols

With the passing of time, signs easily become not only naturalized, but conventionalized as well. Taken out of their original social and historical context, linguistic signs can be emptied of the fullness of their meaning and used as symbolic shorthand. For example, words like 'democracy', 'freedom', 'choice', when uttered by politicians and diplomats, may lose much of their denotative and even their rich connotative meanings, and become political **symbols** in Western democratic rhetoric; signifiers like 'the French Revolution', 'May 68', 'the Holocaust', have simplified an originally confusing amalgam of historical events into conventionalized symbols. The recurrence of these symbols over time creates an accumulation of meaning that not only shapes the memory of sign users but confers to these symbols mythical weight and validity.

The passage of time validates both the sign itself and its users. For signs are reversible; they have the potential of changing the way sign-makers view themselves, and therefore the way they act. The use of signs enables current speakers to place past events into a current context of talk, i.e. to recontextualize past events and thus provide a framework to anticipate, i.e. precontextualize, future events. Ultimately such construction and reconstruction of contexts through the use of signs enables language users to control their environment, and to monitor their and others' behavior in that environment.

We see this controlling effect at work, for example, in the publicity logos, the advertisement jingles of commercial corporations, and in the outward signs of national patriotism, from flags to mottos to mementos (see Chapter 6). Cultural **stereotypes** are frozen signs that affect both those who use them and those whom they serve to characterize. Much of what we call ideology is, in this respect, symbolic language. For example, words like 'rebels' or 'freedom fighters' to denote anti-government forces, 'challenges' or 'problems' to denote obstacles, and 'collaboration' or 'exploitation' to denote workers' labor, are cultural symbols propagated and sustained by sign-makers of different political leanings in their respective discourse communities. The way in which language intersects with social power makes some uses of cultural signs seem legitimate, i.e. natural, others illegitimate, i.e. unnatural and even taboo. A right-wing newspaper, for example, would censor the use of 'freedom fighters' to refer to guerrilla forces; its readers would find it quite natural to see them referred to as 'rebels'.

This last example illustrates the problem encountered throughout this chapter of keeping semantics and pragmatics strictly separate from one another. Where does semantics end and pragmatics begin? The meanings of words as they are linked both to the world and to other words establish a speech community's pool of semantic resources; but this semantic pool is constantly enriched and changed through the use that is made of it in social contexts.

Summary

Signs establish between words and things various semantic relations of **denotation**, **connotation**, or **iconicity** that give general meaning to the world. In addition, signs establish semantic relations with other signs in the direct environment of verbal exchanges, or in the historical context of a discourse community. The creation of meaning through signs is not arbitrary, but is, rather, guided by the human desire for recognition, influence, power, and the general motivation for social and cultural survival. Since meaning is encoded in language with a purpose, meaning as sign is contingent upon the context in which signs are used to regulate human action. Thus it is often difficult to draw a clear line between the generic semantic meanings of the code and the pragmatic meanings of the code in various contexts of use.

3
Meaning as action

After years of searching in vain for the meaning of life in philosophy, law, and theology, Goethe's Dr. Faust decides that meaning is not in words, but in actions. The famous statement in the Bible 'In the beginning was the Word' needs to be replaced, he says, by a statement more appropriate to modern times. 'In the beginning was Action!' he exclaims, and he sells his soul to the Devil. If he does get saved in the end, it is for having accepted that all action is contingent upon the time and place in which it unfolds. Meaning is never achieved once and for all, it must be conquered anew in every utterance through the verbal actions and interactions of speakers and hearers, writers, and readers.

In this chapter we consider the way in which cultural meaning is created through the actions and interactions of speakers in social contexts.

Context of situation, context of culture

It is the study of so-called primitive languages in their respective societal contexts that has put into question Western linguists' exclusive views of language as an instrument of thought, or as Faust would say, as the primary domain of philosophy, law, and theology. The anthropologist Bronislaw Malinowski (1884–1942) was working at describing the fishing and agricultural practices of the native inhabitants of the Trobriand Islands, when he discovered for the first time that their language (Kiriwinian) was the key to understanding the meaning of their practices. But, as he sat on the beach, observing the fishermen cry out from one canoe to the other, manoeuvering their boats across difficult straits, he realized that, in order to understand what was going on, it was not enough to understand and write down the meaning of their words. One had to understand why they said what they said and how they said it to whom in a specific **context of situation**. In addition, one had to link their words, beliefs, and mindsets to a larger **context of culture** such as: tribal economics, social organization, kinship patterns, fertility rites, seasonal rhythms, concepts of time and space. Thus the semantic meanings of verbal signs had to be supplemented by the pragmatic meanings of verbal actions in context.

How is pragmatic meaning culturally realized in verbal exchanges? Meaning is created not only through what speakers say to one another, but through what they *do* with words in order to respond to the demands of their environment. In this chapter, we consider what these responses entail.

Structures of expectation

As discussed in Chapter 1, language users bring to any verbal encounter blueprints for action that have developed through their socialization or acculturation in a given society. From childhood on they have learned to realize certain speech acts in a culturally appropriate manner, like saying 'Thank you' in response to receiving gifts, and 'Goodbye' as a way of closing encounters; they have learned to speak differently to people of different ranks and to distinguish an insult from a compliment. These behaviors have become second nature to them because they are grounded in their physical experience of the phenomena around them. This experience filters their perception and their interpretation of the world.

Language users have not only learned to interpret signs and to act upon them; they have also learned to expect certain behaviors of others as well. In the same manner as they expect cars to stop at a STOP sign and pedestrians to be able to cross the street at a WALK sign, so too they expect to be greeted upon a first encounter, to be listened to when they speak, to have their questions answered. There are cultural differences in these expectations. French speakers from France may expect to be greeted with a handshake, Americans may expect a smile instead; a professor may expect to be greeted differently from a student, a friend from a stranger. On the basis of their experience in their culture (or combination of cultures), people organize knowledge about the world and use this knowledge to predict interpretations and relationships regarding any new information, events, and experiences that come their way. The general **structures of expectation** established in people's minds by the culture they live in have been variously called **frames** or **schemata**.

Contextualization cues, situated inferences

The words people exchange in verbal encounters are linked in a myriad of ways to the situational and cultural context in which they occur. Thus, for example, A's words to B: 'I need to get in there. Can you open the door?' will have meaning for B only if he knows English and is able to grasp the semantic meanings of A's utterance; but, he must also relate the 'I' to the friend he knows and recognize him by his voice and his outward appearance; he must relate the 'there' to a room he knows lies behind the door which he sees from where he is standing; he must recognize that 'the' in 'the door' that A wants opened indicates the same door that he sees; from A's smile, tone and intonation, and from the preceding statement of A's needs, he must understand that this is a justified, friendly request for help and not a fortuitous inquiry. In other words, beyond the semantic meaning of A's individual words, B has to understand how these words relate to the pragmatic context of their utterance. These verbal ('I', 'there', 'the door'), paraverbal (stress and intonation, tempo and laughter) and non-verbal signs (gaze direction, gesture, body posture, tone of voice), that help speakers hint at or clarify or guide their listener's interpretations of what is being said among the infinite range of potentially relevant factors of the context, are called **contextualization cues**.

These cues help listeners make the relevant **situated inferences**, i.e. evoke the cultural background and social expectations necessary to interpret speech. Through the use of contextualization cues, speakers and hearers can convey to each other what their expectations are with respect to the communication they are engaged in. Participants in verbal exchanges have to manage their interpretation of each other's utterances in accordance with how they perceive the situational and cultural context to be on an instant-by-instant basis.

Pragmatic coherence

Efforts to make the words uttered meaningful within the situational and cultural context of the exchange are efforts to establish pragmatic **coherence**. Coherence is not given in speakers' utterances, it is created in the minds of speakers and hearers by the inferences they make based on the words they hear. Thus, whereas semantic cohesion relates word to word (see chapter 2), pragmatic coherence relates speaker to speaker within the larger cultural context of communication.

The speaker's efforts to establish pragmatic coherence through the use of contextualization cues can have an inclusionary effect, such as in the following exchange among friends:

Chad: I go out a lot
Deborah: I go out and eat
Peter: You go out? The trouble with ME is if I don't prepare and eat well, I eat a LOT … Because it's not satisfying. And so if I'm just eating like cheese and crackers, I'll just STUFF myself on cheese and crackers. But if I fix myself something nice, I don't have to eat that much.
Deborah: Oh yeah?
Peter: I've noticed that, yeah.
Deborah: Hmmm … Well then it works, then it's a good idea
Peter: It's a good idea in terms of eating, it's not a good idea in terms of time.

(Tannen, Deborah. *Talking Voices. Repetition, Dialogue, Imagery.* Cambridge: Cambridge University Press 1989, page 71)

Through a remarkable crisscross of lexical and phonological repetitions (I go out a lot—I go out and eat—I eat a lot), that gives their talk semantic cohesiveness, Deborah and Peter, who both share the same New York Jewish culture, reinforce each other's cues. The semantic cohesion of the words the speakers utter, combined with a shared cultural background, establishes a deep pragmatic coherence through what the speakers do. The way they echo each other, piggyback on each other's words and phrases, continue each other's sentences, leads each one to infer that what is important in this conversation is not so much the information their words convey (which in fact shows that they disagree with one another), but their sense of being on the same conversational wavelength and belonging to the same culture.

Contextualization cues can also serve to highlight the discrepancies in participants' inferences and frames of expectations, and thus lead to coherence breakdowns in cross-cultural encounters:

> An African-American student has been sent to interview a black housewife in a low-income, inner-city neighborhood. The contact has been made over the phone by someone in the office. The student arrives, rings the bell, and is met by the husband, who opens the door, smiles, and steps towards him:
>
> Husband: So y're gonna check out ma ol lady, hah?
> Student: Ah, no. I only came to get some information. They called from the office.
>
> (Husband, dropping his smile, disappears without a word and calls his wife.)
>
> (Gumperz, John J. *Discourse Strategies.* Cambridge: Cambridge University Press 1982, page 133)

Failing to infer from the husband's stylistic cues (intonation, pronunciation typical of Black English Vernacular, lexical choice of 'ol lady' instead of 'wife', 'check out' instead of 'visit')—the husband's offered solidarity from one African-American to another, the student responds in White Standard English ('I' instead of /a/, 'get' instead of /gi::t/), thereby showing that he is from an academic culture that is not the husband's. The student later reported that the interview that followed was stiff and quite unsatisfactory. Being black himself, he knew he had 'blown it'. However, as we shall see in Chapter 6, the issue is not just one of recognizing contextualizing cues appropriately. In this case, the student had to choose between his identity as an African-American and his identity as a professional academic. The two may have seemed to him incommensurable at the time, and for the sake of sounding professionally reliable he might have felt he had to forego sounding ethnically trustworthy.

Between people from different national cultures, the same contextualization cues may lead to different inferences and may occasion serious misunderstandings, since they tend to be attributed to personal attitudes or character traits. The resulting lack of pragmatic coherence generally leaves the participants baffled and perplexed, or frustrated and angry. Thus, in an encounter at the bank between an Asian customer and a British cashier, the unexpected tone of voice and emphases of the Asian-English speaker may lead to misunderstanding and frustration on the part of the British-English speaker:

Customer: Excuse me
Cashier: Yes sir
Customer: I want to deposit some MOney.
Cashier: Oh. I see. OK. You'll need a deposit form then.
Customer: Yes. NO, NO. This is the WRONG one.

(Gumperz, John J., T. C. Jupp, and Celia Roberts. *Cross-Talk. A Study of Cross Cultural Communication*. London: The National Centre for Industrial Language Training 1977, page 21)

The Asian-English speaker's voice rises and falls on 'some MOney' and this word is also marked by loudness, whereas a British-English speaker's voice would be lowered on 'money' and the emphasis might be on 'deposit'. Using his own system of interpretation, a British-English speaker might think the Asian-English speaker is stating the obvious and might associate his tone of voice with pushiness, where an Asian cashier would not hear this sentence as either rude or pushy. In turn, the Asian-English customer may make the wrong inferences about the British-English speaking cashier:

Cashier: Sorry?
Customer: I got my account in WEMbley
Cashier: Oh you need a GIro form then
Customer: Yes GIro form
Cashier: Why didn't you say so first time?
Customer: Sorry. Didn't KNOW.

Cashier: All RIGHT?
Customer: Thank you

(ibidem)

Tone of voice is usually interpreted as a direct cue to attitude, and therefore, a piece of intended behavior. The Asian customer may hear the cashier's emphasis on the word 'GIro' as indicating an over-emotional and irritated reaction, and his emphasis on 'All RIGHT?' as indicating rude dismissal.

The study of contextualization cues not only brings to light the way in which speakers give pragmatic coherence to their respective utterances; it also gives us a hint at the way participants in verbal interactions co-construct cultural roles for themselves while they co-operatively construct the topic of the conversation.

The co-operative principle

The misunderstandings illustrated in the last example can cause particular frustration because people make the general assumption that verbal exchanges will conform to what the philosopher Paul Grice has referred to as the **co-operative principle**. People can generally assume that in conversations in which, for example, the exchange of information is primary, speakers will not say more than is necessary for the purpose of the exchange and will say all that is necessary to convey the information required. They generally expect that what their interlocutor says is relevant to the topic at hand; that her message will be clear and understandable; and under normal circumstances she will not state something she doesn't believe to be true. The expectations of speakers and hearers in informational exchanges are in part shaped by these four maxims of the co-operative principle in conversation. If listeners are sometimes frustrated because they feel that their interlocutor is trying to give them unnecessary or irrelevant information, to avoid the topic, or worse, to deceive them, that is because they expect him/her to abide by the maxims for co-operative behavior.

Speakers from different cultural backgrounds may have different interpretations of what it means to be true, relevant, brief or clear with regard to conversations. They may have different definitions of the speech activity itself. A service encounter at the bank might have a different social value in India and in England, and the roles of cashier and customer might be differently defined. But they all enter a verbal exchange assuming that there will be some sort of co-operation between the parties involved.

Participants' roles and the co-construction of culture

In addition to the institutional roles that speakers assume by virtue of their occupation or their status (for example, bank teller, customer, teacher, pupil), there are also local participant roles, or participation frameworks, according to the sociologist Erving Goffman, that all speakers and hearers must carve out for themselves through what they say and the way they say it. Through their register (informal, formal), their key or tone of voice (serious, jesting, sarcastic), the frequency of their interruptions, the way they take the floor, the feedback signals they give, their choice of lexical and grammatical structures, the distribution of their silences, participants in verbal exchanges play out various social roles that reveal a great deal about the social persona they wish to represent, and about the social personae they are thereby assigning to their interlocutors. For example, they may come across as confident or shy, interested or indifferent, close or distant, helpful or pushy; they may take on a friendly, competitive, bossy, motherly role.

They may take on various interactional roles as well. For example, consider the following interaction between A (male, husband), B (female, A's wife), and C (female, friend and neighbor):

A: Y'want a piece of candy?
B: No =
C: = She's on a diet

(Schiffrin, Deborah. *Approaches to Discourse*. London: Basil Blackwell 1994, page 107)

C is in a sense animating words that are not hers, but B's. By speaking for B, she might be perceived as either 'chipping in' in a helpful manner, or 'butting in' and not minding her own business. Her intervention at this point, latched on to B's rejection of A's offer, can be viewed as a cue to B and C's relationship and their relationship to A. C happens to be a long-time friend and neighbor of B; her utterance can therefore be understood as enacting B's role as helpful explainer of B's refusal, with the intention of minimizing the negative impact that B's rejection might have on A. In other contexts, speaking for another person might be viewed as signalling not solidarity, but, rather, an asymmetrical relationship of power and authority, such as when a mother speaks for her child, a husband for his wife, a teacher for a student.

Speaking for another or animating his/her words is one of the many roles participants can take *vis-à-vis* their words and those of others. Another role may be that of principal, i.e. talking by virtue of the institutional power granted the speaker by society. A third possible role is that of author, i.e. assuming responsibility for what one says. Speakers may often speak both as authors and as principals. In the example above, A offers B some candy both as a responsible user of the English language and as one who has the legitimate authority to offer candy to friends and family. Listeners in turn may be acknowledged or non-acknowledged participants playing a variety of roles: addressees, hearers, eavesdroppers, bystanders. Here B, A's wife, is the addressee; C, the visitor, is a ratified hearer.

It is through the enactment of these roles that culture is jointly constructed through language in action. For example, children are not only biological entities, but socially constituted roles, i.e. children are culturally constituted *as children* by parents who consistently 'speak for them', and by children who accept to be 'spoken for', as in the following well-known example:

Kathryn: Mommy sock. /de/ - dirty.
Mother: Yes. They're all dirty. I know.

(Bloom, Lois M. *One Word at a Time*. The Hague: Mouton 1970, page 47).

The infant, who cannot speak properly yet (from the Latin *in-fans*: the one who does not speak), has to be spoken for by the mother, who speaks what she understands the child to mean. The same can be said of pupils whose words are animated and evaluated by teachers. Pupils' and teachers' membership in school culture is recognizable in part by the way teachers tend to animate pupils' utterances, as shown in the example below, where a teacher and her class are talking about apples:

Teacher: What color are the pips?
Child 1: Brown
Child 2: Black
Child 1: Brown
Child 2: Brown
Teacher: Yes they're dark brown that's right.

(Wells, Gordon *Learning Through Interaction*. Cambridge: Cambridge University Press 1981, page 217)

Similarly, gender roles are not the natural result of biological makeup, but they, too, are socially constructed by males and females enacting different participant roles in conversation. These roles are achieved by a pattern of small cues that show either self-assertiveness or uncertainty, dominance or submissiveness, and that get attributed over time to one gender or another. Consider the following:

Husband: When will dinner be ready?
Wife: Oh … around six o'clock …?

(Lakoff, Robin. *Language and Woman's Place*. New York: Farrar, Straus, and Giroux 1976, page 17)

The woman's rising intonation is often interpreted as signaling female uncertainty and lack of self-assertiveness (or, on the contrary, female considerateness). Compare the following:

Female: So uh you really can't bitch when you've got all those on the same day (4.2) but I uh asked my physics professor if I couldn't chan ⌐ ge that ⌐
Male: └ Don't ┘ touch that
Female: What?
Male: I've got everything jus' how I want it in that notebook you'll screw it up leafin' through it like that

(West, Candace and Don H. Zimmerman. 'Small Insults: A study of interruptions in cross-sex conversations between unacquainted persons'. In B. Thorne, C. Kramarae, and N. Henley (Eds.) *Language, Gender and Society.* Newbury House 1983, page 105).

The male's interruption may be viewed as a sign of male dominance, his power to switch the topic to suit his own agenda. However, one may not automatically equate a participant's role with the gender of an individual before one has observed that individual behave in various contexts with various interlocutors of both similar and different gender.

Language use is a cultural act not only because it reflects the ways in which one individual acts on another individual through such speech acts as thanking, greeting, complimenting, that are variously accomplished in various cultures. Language use is a cultural act because its users co-construct the very social roles that define them as members of a discourse community.

Summary

The system of signs that constitute culture is actively constructed through the verbal actions taken by sign-makers in interaction with one another. In the construction of meaning, the interpretation of events is grounded in each person's experience and field of perception. The context of situation and the context of culture in which verbal actions take place are constitutive of these actions; they imbue them with the necessary pragmatic coherence. As they talk, speakers draw on frames of expectations they have in common with other members of the group who share the same life history and the same larger context of culture. Based on these expectations, speakers then position themselves vis-a-vis the situational context of a given exchange by means of context-ualization cues. These contextualization cues are evidence of situated inferences that speakers make, based on their culturally shared frames of expectations and applied to the local situation of the exchange. These cues give the exchange pragmatic coherence. The participants maintain this verbal coherence by observing a principle of conversational co-operation, that prompts them to align their expectations onto those of others by playing various participant roles. All these actions by the participants are finely attuned to the cultural norms and conventions of the group they belong to and to its attitudes and beliefs.

However, the meanings of words are different if they are conveyed face-to-face in the close proximity of another fellow human being, or over a distance, through the technologized medium of writing and print. In the next two chapters we examine the features of orality and literacy in relation to language and culture.

4
Spoken language, oral culture

We saw in the last chapter how participants in verbal interactions carve out for themselves and for each other a cultural space of reference in which they take up various social roles. In this chapter and the next we explore further how social structure is constructed through the two very different media of speech and writing.

The spoken medium is directly linked to the time of its enunciation and to the perception by those present of the transient dimensions of the verbal event. By contrast, the technology of writing, as a spatial extension of the mind and the hand, has been able to overcome the ephemeral, auditory nature of spoken language by translating it into more permanent, visible signs on a page. We first discuss the differences between the two media.

Speech and writing

It is difficult, if not impossible, for us to experience what members of exclusively oral cultures must have experienced before the invention of writing; the very term **orality** is defined over against the written word and was coined by **literate** people within a context of **literacy**. Even illiterate people nowadays live in a world whose consciousness has been totally transformed by the advent of writing and, later, of print. Primary orality, then, can never be recovered. However, traces of orality have remained both in speech and in writing—**orate** features of language use that hark back to the primary orality of pre-writing times. From these traces, scholars have identified the following seven characteristics of conversational speech as distinguished from expository writing.

1 Speech is transient, rather than permanent. Because of physical constraints, interlocutors may not speak at the same time, or else they cannot hear what the others say. They are bound by the non-reversible distribution of turns at talk. Written language, by contrast, can be stored, retrieved, and recollected, and responses can be delayed. Because it cannot be immediately challenged as in oral communication, written language carries more weight and hence more prestige. Moreover, the permanence of writing as a medium can easily lead people to suppose that what it expresses is permanent too, hence the important link between written documents and the law.

2 Speech is additive or 'rhapsodic'. Because of the dialogic nature of oral interaction, speakers 'rhapsodize', i.e. stitch together elements from previous turns-at-talk, they add language as they go along (and ... and, then ... and then ...), thus showing conversational co-operation in the building of their own turn. By contrast, the information conveyed in writing is hierarchically ordered within the clause structure, and is linearly arranged on the page, from left to right, right to left, or top to bottom, according to the cultural convention. Since it is likely to be read by distant, unknown, or yet-to-be-born audiences, it has developed an information structure characterized by a high level of cohesion.

3 Speech is aggregative, i.e. it makes use of verbal aggregates or formulaic expressions, ready-made chunks of speech that maintain the contact between interlocutors, also called **phatic communion**. By contrast, in the absence of such direct contact and for the sake of economy of information over long distances or long periods of time, and because it can be read and re-read at will, writing has come to be viewed as the medium that fosters analysis, logical reasoning and abstract categorization.

4 Speech is redundant or 'copious'. Because speakers are never quite sure whether their listener is listening, paying attention, comprehending and remembering what they are saying or not, they tend to make frequent use of repetition, paraphrase, and

restatement. By contrast, since written language doesn't have to make such demands on short-term memory, it tends to avoid redundancy.

5 Speech is loosely structured grammatically and is lexically sparse; writing, by contrast, is grammatically compact and lexically dense. What does this mean concretely? Speakers have to attend to many aspects of the situation while they concentrate on what they are saying, and while they monitor the way they are saying it. Thus, their speech is characterized by false starts, filled and unfilled pauses, hesitations, parenthetic remarks, unfinished sentences. They create their utterances as they are speaking them. One way of keeping control of this balancing act is to use grammatical resources as best serves one's immediate needs, and to leave the vocabulary as sparse as possible. Writers, by contrast, have time to pack as much information in the clause as they can, using all the complex syntactic resources the language can give them; they can condense large quantities of information in a tighter space by using, for example, dense nominalized phrases. The contrast is shown in the examples below.

WRITTEN	SPOKEN
Every previous visit had left me with a sense of the futility of further action on my part.	'Whenever I'd visited there before, I'd ended up feeling that it would be futile if I tried to do anything more.'
Improvements in technology have reduced the risks and high costs associated with simultaneous installation	'Because the technology has improved, it's less risky than it used to be when you install them at the same time, and it doesn't cost so much either.'

(Halliday, M.A.K. *Spoken and Written Language*. Oxford University Press 1985, page 81)

6 Speech tends to be **people-centered**, writing tends to be **topic-centered**. Because of the presence of an audience and the need to keep the conversation going, speakers not only focus on their topic, but try to engage their listeners as well, and appeal to

their senses and emotions. In expository writing, by contrast, the topic or message and its transferability from one context to the other is the main concern. Writers of expository prose try to make their message as clear, unambiguous, coherent, and trustworthy as possible since they will not always be there to explain and defend it. Of course, other written texts, in particular of the literary or promotional kind, appeal to the readers' emotions, and display many features characteristic of speech.

7 Speech, being close to the situation at hand, is **context dependent**; writing, being received far from its original context of production, is **context-reduced**. Because of the **dialogic** character of oral exchanges, truth in the oral mode is jointly constructed and based on commonsense experience. Truth in the literate mode is based on the logic and the coherence of the argument being made.

The features listed above are not inherent in the spoken or in the written medium. Orality and literacy have to be seen on a continuum of more or less 'orate', more or less literate uses of both spoken and written language. A scribbled memo, an e-mail, an informal letter, like a conversation or a homily, are written in the orate mode; an academic lecture, a scientific presentation, like a scholarly article, are spoken in the literate mode. And a poem like the Emily Dickinson poem we started out with (see Chapter 1), has both orate and literate features, as we shall see in the next chapter.

Moreover, as has been hotly debated in recent years, the cognitive skills associated with literacy are not intrinsic to the technology of writing. Although the written medium does have its own physical parameters, there is nothing in alphabet and script that would make them more suited, say, for logical and analytic thinking than the spoken medium. To understand why literacy has become associated with logic and analysis, one needs to understand the historical association of the invention of the Greek alphabet with Plato's philosophy, and the influence of Plato's dichotomy between ideas and language on the whole of Western thought. It is cultural and historical contingency, not technology *per se*, that determines the way we think, but technology serves to enhance and give power to one way of thinking over another. Technology is always linked to power, as power is linked to dominant cultures.

We now turn to the cultural matrix of language as it is used in verbal exchanges. We look in particular at how the social structure of a discourse community is reflected, constructed, and perpetuated by the way its members use language to define their position *vis-à-vis* others, to save each other's social face, and in general to 'language' their experience in a style appropriate to the conventions of the group.

Indicating status

In verbal encounters, what people say to each other, for example, A: 'Bill, why don't you meet me here tomorrow?' is anchored in the perspective of speaker A, as evidenced in this case by the words 'you', 'me', 'here', 'tomorrow', also called **deictics**. Markers of **social deixis** give an indication not only of where the speaker stands in time and place—namely in a 'today' in the 'here' of speaking—but also of his/her status within the social structure, and of the status the speaker gives the addressee. For example, the use of *vous* or *tu* in French, *Sie* or *du* in German can **index** either power or solidarity, distance or closeness. English used to have 'you' for distance, 'thou' for closeness; now English has only retained the 'you', but social deixis in English expresses social position by other forms of address like 'Bill', 'Bill X', 'Mister X', 'Professor X' and the like. These forms of address index social class, as in the use of *vous* between parents and between parents and children that can still be found in some upper-class French families; they can also index a generational culture, as the currently prevalent use of reciprocal *tu* or *Du* among students or young people in France and Germany; they can also index a culture that wants itself to be egalitarian and democratic as in the informal forms of address used in the United States ('dear friend', 'call me Bill'). The police's use of a non-reciprocal *tu* to address North African youth in France expresses an explicit display of power; being addressed with *tu* indexes the subordinate or marginal place occupied by these youths in French society today.

Social positionings

The use of social deictics like pronouns, forms of address, or names, is one way speakers align themselves to the cultural context as they understand it. We have seen in Chapter 3 how changes in intonation and pronunciation can also indicate changes in our perception of our role as a participant in an interaction, and in our alignment to others. Goffman called such a positioning **footing**, i.e. the stance we take up to ourselves and to the others present as expressed in the way we manage the production or reception of utterances. A change in footing is usually marked by a change in register, tone of voice or bodily orientation. For example, it is frequently the case in the United States that a Northerner talking to a Southerner instinctively aligns his/her way of talking on that of the Southerner, as a sign of conversational co-operation; similarly, a native speaker who starts adopting a style of speaking called 'foreigner talk' when talking to a foreigner, shows a convergence that can be interpreted, as we shall see further in Chapter 6, either as cultural solidarity or as the display of cultural power. We can see this same phenomenon occurring in classrooms. A teacher talks differently to her pupils when she addresses them as a class or as individual children:

1   Now listen everybody

2   At ten o'clock we'll have assembly. We'll all go out together and go to the auditorium and sit in the first two rows. Mr. Dock, the principal, is going to speak to us. When he comes in, sit quietly and listen carefully.

3   Don't wiggle your legs. Pay attention to what I'm saying.

(Goffman, Erving. *Forms of Talk*. Philadelphia: University of Pennsylvania Press 1981, page 127)

The switch in tone and in the use of pronouns from 'everybody' to 'we' to 'you' and 'I' clearly sets the utterances 1, 2, and 3 apart from one another. Three different footings are involved here: the first statement is a claim on the children's immediate behavior, the second is a review of experiences to come, and the third a side remark to a particular child. The teacher, as a speaker, switches roles from being a principal (in the legalistic sense), i.e. representing the institutional voice of the school, to being an animator or class teacher who animates her students' voices through the (euphemistic) use of 'we', to becoming an author or private adult demanding to be listened to. The switch in register indexes a switch in cultural alignment, from marking the teacher's membership in the institutional culture of the school to her identity as an individual speaker, albeit endowed with the authority of an adult. Both switches, in tone and in register, index a distinct change in footing.

Defining one's footing can also be achieved through **code-switching**. In a famous passage of *The Magic Mountain*, Thomas Mann's German hero, Hans Castorp, gets acquainted with the seductive Russian Asian guest, Clawdia Chauchat, in the high-altitude environment of a Swiss sanatorium. It is in this remote location, far away from any fixed cultural conventions, and with the freedom granted by carnival night, that Hans Castorp dares address Madame Chauchat with *du*:

- 'Hast du vielleicht einen Bleistift?'
- 'Ich? … Ja, vielleicht … Du bist sehr ehrgeizig … Du bist … sehr eifrig … Voilà! … '
- 'Siehst du wohl, ich wußte doch, daß du einen haben würdest.'
- 'Prenez garde, il est un peu fragile', sagte sie. 'C'est à visser, tu sais.'
- [(German) Do you happen to have a pencil?
- Me? Perhaps I have … You are so eager … you are … very ambitious … (French) There!
- (German) You see, I knew you would have one.
- (French) Take care, it is a little fragile, (German) she said. (French) It is meant to be screwed, you know.]

(Mann, Thomas. *Der Zauberberg*. Frankfurt: Fischer 1956, page 305)

With this initial switch from the more distant *vous*-form to the more intimate *du/tu*-form, and with the unrestrained switch between German and French, the German engineer and the Russian aristocrat find a common cultural ground that Castorp uses to declare his love to her in French. These changes in footing help the young German hero to confront his inability to choose between the Western and the Eastern influences on his German soul and to find his own identity as a German (see Chapter 6).

Not all changes in footing are as dramatic as this one; but they all correspond to a change in the way we perceive events. A change in footing is connected with a change in our frame for events. As we saw in Chapter 3, framing, or the ability to apply a frame of interpretation to an utterance or speech event through a contextualization cue (in this case the switch in social deictic and in code), is our way of linking the speech event to other similar speech events we have experienced, and to anticipate future events. It is by sharing frames of interpretation that people know that they share the same culture.

Here are, as an example, two different frames established at the beginning of two group discussions, one conducted in English by American students, one conducted in Japanese by Japanese students.

In answer to the question 'Why did you decide to study Japanese?' the American students began their discussion as follows:

Jenny:	I hate ⎤ ⎡ Oops
Teacher:	⎣ Go ahead ⎦
	(pause 3.5 seconds; sounds of opening and closing a door as teacher leaves the discussion room)
Beth:	Okay::
Mike:	So, Beth, why ⎡ did you decide to learn Japanese
Sean:	⎣ Why.
Beth:	Uhm ... I guess I decided to learn Japanese because (Beth continues)

(Watanabe, Suwako. 'Cultural differences in framing: American and Japanese group discussions.' In Tannen, D. *Framing in Discourse*. Oxford University Press 1993, page 182)

In the 3.5 seconds pause, the alignment of the participants changed from a pre-discussion frame to that of a discussion frame. Beth's 'Okay' signals the onset of that discussion frame, seen as an instructional task to be dealt with as efficiently as possible. By framing the verbal exchange in this manner, the American students are perpetuating a discussion style typical of

American academic culture, in which a problem or a question posed at the outset gets tackled without further ado by whoever takes the initiative to start the discussion.

By contrast, when asked to discuss the question 'Why did you decide to study abroad?', the Japanese students began their discussion as follows (English translation):

Teacher: Then, please
Yasuo: let's see, as you see, uhm, basically we'll follow the number
Keiko: that's right. Number one, number
Fumiko: h-h-h-h
two, and number three.
Yasuo: Hm. It's easy to get in.
Keiko: That's right. then …
well, the top one, each one of us has to talk in turn, I wonder.
Fumiko: That is so.
Yasuo: That's right … following numbers, how are we going to do …
Ikuo: Ladies first
Fumiko: Please
Yasuo: Oh, that sounds good.
Fumiko: [laugh]
Keiko: [laugh]
Keiko: Then, from the younger one [laugh]
Fumiko: Please [laugh]
Fumiko: No. No. Big sister. [laugh]
Keiko: What?
Ikuo: It doesn't matter, does it.
Keiko: As you see, [Keiko takes turn]

(ibidem, pages 184–5)

Through this elaborate framing exercise it seems that the Japanese speakers were negotiating not only the procedural aspects of the subsequent discussion, but also a hierarchical order within the group. The question of who speaks first is, in Japanese culture, of paramount importance. No one simply decided to speak first, as in the American groups. In all the Japanese group discussions, a female member started, followed by the other female member, then by the younger male member, and last by the oldest male member. Without establishing first the participants' social positions, the speakers would not have known which language style and vocabulary to choose. And one result of failing to use an appropriate linguistic form is loss of face. By framing the task with an elaborate discussion on procedural matters, the Japanese participants enacted and perpetuated a Japanese culture that is particularly sensitive to the mutual need to save social face (see the next section). But they also replicated the Japanese culture of talkshows, interviews, and casual forum/roundtable-type discussions, commonly set up by the media in order to elicit personalized stories. In other words, they enacted both the structure of their society, and the demands of the speech event as their culture perceives its genre to be.

Protecting face

The ultimate aim of negotiating frames and footings in conversation is to protect one's own and other participants' **face** at all times. For, the co-operative principle we discussed in the last chapter is less a guide to individual behavior than it is the very condition of continued social interaction, and the enactment of a group's cultural self-understanding.

Members of a cultural group need to feel respected and not impinged upon in their autonomy, pride, and self-sufficiency (negative face). They also need to be reinforced in their view of themselves as polite, considerate, respectful members of their culture (positive face). These two contradictory needs require delicate facework, since it is in the interest of all participants in a verbal exchange that everyone maintain both his/her negative and positive face, so that the exchange can continue. In the example given above for the Japanese group, the one who speaks first is the one who runs the greatest risk of face loss, because he/she has to take the floor without knowing where the others stand. The turn-taking order is thus indirectly arranged so that juniors and inferiors take earlier turns, perhaps because their face is considered less important, while seniors/superiors take later turns.

The negotiation of frames and footings and the **facework** accomplished in verbal encounters among members of a given social group gives rise to group-specific discourse styles. In particular, as we shall see below, what distinguish people from different cultures are the different ways they use orate and literate discourse styles in various speech genres for various social purposes.

Conversational style

In face-to-face verbal exchanges, the choice of orate features of speech can give the participants a feeling of joint interpersonal involvement rather than the sense of detachment or objectivity that comes with the mere transmission of factual information. Different contexts of situation and different contexts of culture call for different **conversational styles**.

Compare for example an interview, in which the purpose is to elicit information, and a conversation among friends, where the purpose is to share past experiences.

Interview between journalist and young apprentice in Germany:
A: and where do you work?
B: I work in the metal industry
A: uhuh … why did you choose that particular job? in the metal industry?
B: well … it was … so to speak … the job of my dreams. I wanted to work, but not particularly an intellectual job, but a more physical one
A: so … you can say that you chose that job yourself?
B: I chose that job myself

(Kramsch, Claire. *Discourse Analysis and Second Language Teaching*. Washington, D.C.: Center for Applied Linguistics 1981, page 62)

From the controlled, non-overlapping sequence of turns, the interviewer's attempt at professional, detached, objectivity, the cautious responses of the young apprentice desirous to be forthcoming with the required information, we recognize the typical style of a speech event called 'interview'. This literate journalistic style is quite different from the orate style one may find in a conversation among friends:

Conversation between Peter and Deborah, both from a New York Jewish cultural background:

Peter: What I've been doing is cutting down on my sleep
Deborah: Oy! ⌐ [*sighs*]
Peter: └And I've been ... and I ⌐s
Deborah: └I do that too but it's
              painful. ⌐
Peter: └Yeah. Fi:ve, six hours a night,
              and ⌐
Deborah: └Oh God how can you do it. You survive?

(Tannen, Deborah. *Conversational Style. Analyzing Talk Among Friends*. Norwood, N.J.: Ablex 1984, page 82)

Here, Peter and Deborah's common cultural background is enacted through a distinctive orate conversational style, where paralinguistic signals like sighs and interjections ('oy!') signal empathy, the heavy use of personal pronouns ('I', 'you') indexes both ego involvement and involvement with the listener, and where frequent interruptions and overlaps index a high degree of conversational co-operation. Note, however, that this is how Deborah herself interprets these phenomena. Interlocutors from another culture with a more literate conversational style, marked by brevity, conciseness, and a concern for exactitude, might interpret the overlaps, the frequent backchannel signals and the interjections not as co-operation, but on the contrary as so many violations of their conversational space. They might perceive Deborah and Peter as being intolerable blabberers and might in turn be perceived by them as being standoffish and unsociable.

The orate–literate continuum gets realized differently in different cultural genres, like interviews and friendly conversations, but also in different cultural traditions within one genre, such as classroom talk. For example, Indian children from the Warm Springs reservation in Oregon, who are used to learning by silently listening to and watching adults in their family, and by participating in social events within the community as a whole, have a notably different interactional behavior in the classroom than their Anglo-American peers and the teacher, even though all speak English. They mostly remain silent, do not respond to direct solicitations to display their knowledge in public, do not vie for the attention of the teacher, and seem more interested in working together with their peers.

No doubt people are able to display a variety of conversational styles in various situations, and one should avoid equating one person or one culture with one discourse style. For example, Deborah and Peter are perfectly capable of adopting a literate discourse style in interview situations, and Warm Spring Indian children can be very lively conversationalists when among peers outside the classroom. However, by temperament and upbringing, people do tend to prefer one or the other style in a given situation. This style, in turn, forms part of their cultural identity and sense of self, as we shall see in Chapter 6.

If all conversational styles are equally valid, since they reflect the equally respectable values of the discourse communities they come from, not all styles have equal power, as women and ethnic minorities have long discovered. The problem in education, in particular, is how to combine different sets of values, different discourse and learning styles so as not to suppress anyone's sense of worth, yet give everyone access to a dominant conversational style imposed by forces outside the local communities' control.

Narrative style

The influence of culture on discourse style also becomes apparent in the differential distribution of orate and literate features of speech in story telling. For example, using the short 'pear narrative' film by William Chafe, Tannen asked native speakers from Anglo-American and Greek background to retell the film in their own words. Here is how Tannen tells the film:

It showed a man picking pears from a tree, then descending and dumping them into one of three baskets on the ground. A boy comes by on a bicycle and steals a basket of pears. As he's riding away, he passes a girl on a bike, his hat flies off his head, and the bike overturns. Three boys appear and help him gather his pears. They find his hat and return it to him and he gives them pears. The boys then pass the farmer who has just come down from the tree and discovered that his basket of pears is missing. He watches them walk by eating pears.

(Tannen, Deborah. 'What's in a Frame?' in *Framing in Discourse*. Oxford University Press 1993, page 21).

In comparing the narratives told by American women in English and Greek women in Greek, Tannen reports that each group had a distinctive **narrative style**. The Greeks told 'better stories', by often interweaving judgments about the character's behavior (for example, the boy should not have stolen the pears or should have thanked his helpers sooner), or about the film's message (for example, that it showed a slice of agricultural life, or that little children help each other). In contrast, the Americans reportedly gave a 'better recollection' of the original sequence of events, and gave all the details they could remember. They used their judgment to comment on the filmmaker's technique (for example, that the costumes were unconvincing or the soundtrack out of proportion). The Greeks seemed to draw upon an interactive experience which was focused more on interpersonal involvement: telling the story in ways that would interest the interviewer, interpreting the film's human message. The Americans seemed to draw on their willingness to approach a school task for its own demands. They were focusing on the content of the film, treating it as a cinematic object, with critical objectivity. Each group made differential use of orate and literate features according to the expectations their culture had prepared them to have of the task at hand.

It would be dangerous, of course, to generalize this example to all Greeks and all Americans, or to suggest that Greeks in general tell better stories than Americans. As we discussed in Chapter 1, every culture is heterogeneous, i.e. it is composed of a variety of subcultures, and every situation elicits a variety of responses, even within the same national culture. The only conclusion one can draw from examples such as this one is that, given the same situation and the same task, people from different cultures will interpret the situation and the demands of the task differently, and thus behave in different ways. Nevertheless, because the definition of what makes a 'good' story varies from culture to culture, we can expect storytellers to conform to those models of the genre that were available to them in the culture they grew up in.

Summary

The ways in which language means, both as sign and as action, differ according to the medium used. The spoken medium, in particular, bears the marks of more or less orality, more or less literacy, as measured against the characteristic features of conversational-spoken vs. essayist-written language. Cultures themselves are more or less orate, more or less literate according to the uses their members make of the spoken and the written language in various contexts. Through the social organization of talk, culture is constructed across day-to-day dialogues, through the choice of frames and footings that speakers adopt *vis-à-vis* their own and others' discourse, and through the way they collaborate in the necessary facework within a variety of discourse types. Culture puts its imprint on the conversational and narrative styles of the members of a social group. These styles are generally considered to form part of people's cultural identities.

5

Print language, literate culture

The technology of writing and print technology have over time not only changed the medium of language use, but irrevocably changed our way of thinking and talking about culture. This chapter will deal with issues of text, power, and the cultural politics of literacy.

Written language, textual culture

We first need to take an historical perspective on the way technology has affected the relationship of language and culture. The invention of writing around 3000 BC transformed oral tradition, transmitted through storytelling, bardic epics, mythical re-enactments and performances, into textual tradition, handed down by scribes. The culture of the text, as exemplified in the Chinese scribal culture, passed on its wisdom not through reading, but through the faithful copying of texts. It was through the rewriting of fixed texts in one's own handwriting that the truths of the ancestors got embodied anew into new generations. Copying texts was the major way of getting at the texts' meaning, and of obtaining the social prestige that came with a literate education.

The culture of the text and its respect for and obedience to textual authority was also central to the Judaic and early Christian traditions. In these cultures, revelation was to take place through commentary, exegesis, and translation. The implication was that through the study and interpretation of the sacred texts it would be possible to recover the original truths dispensed in oral form by God, angels, and the prophets. The simultaneous desirability and impossibility of that goal have been the subject of many a scholar's concern. It was the ultimate focus of the Kabbalah, a twelfth-century school of Jewish mysticism named after the Hebrew term for 'literary tradition'. What Kabbalists looked for in the Bible was not primarily philosophical ideas, but a symbolic description of the hidden process of divine life. Viewing written language itself as a micro-representation of the universe, Kabbalists built an elaborate system of meanings based on numbers and the letters of the Hebrew alphabet, in an effort to accede to the unwritten secrets of the universe. So, for example, the four letters of the Hebrew name of God, *Yod he vav he* (*Yahweh*), have in Hebrew the numerical value forty-five from their position in the alphabet, as does the word 'Adam'. From this linguistic fact, Kabbalists drew the conclusion that God is in fact Adam. The god who can be apprehended by man is himself, they claimed, the First Man. One can readily see why the Catholic Church condemned the Kabbalah as a heresy.

Textual cultures illustrate the dilemma represented by the invention of writing. As we saw in Chapter 1, writing permits record-keeping, and thus can be an aid to memory; by fixing the fluidity of speech, it makes tradition into scripture, which can then be easily codified and made into a norm, a canon, or a law. But writing, uprooted from its original context through the passing of time and through its dissemination in space, increases also the absurdity of the quest for the one true 'original' meaning. Ancient texts can only be understood though the multiple meanings given to them by latter-day commentators, exegetes, translators. Even legal documents, that try to control and legislate people's lives, have to be re-interpreted anew for every particular case.

Print and power

Institutional power has traditionally ensured cultural continuity by providing a safeguard against the unbounded interpretation of texts. In medieval times, monks, scribes, and commentators served as the gate-keepers and interpreters of tradition against cultural change. With the advent of **print culture**, the need to hand copy texts disappeared, and so did the caste of scribes. At the same time, ecclesiastical authority itself was on the wane. The combination of Gutenberg's invention of the printing press around 1440, and the translation of the Bible into vernacular German by Martin Luther in 1522, made the sacred truths accessible to all, and not only to the Church-educated elite. It opened the door to the unlimited and uncontrolled proliferation of meanings. Soon, the Church monopoly on meaning was replaced by the interpretive authority and censorship of secular powers, i.e. the academy, the press, and the political institutions. Whereas oral culture has been seen as exerting a 'prophylactic', or invisible, censorship on its members through the conservative pressure of the social group; textual culture, because it is more able to express the particular meanings of individual writers, has usually been censored by external powers, like the Church or the State. Thus, while the written medium has been viewed as potentially more subversive than the spoken medium, in reality it has also been constrained by institutions like the academy, the law, the publishing industry, that have always been in control of new technologies.

The academic monopoly over the meaning of written texts has manifested itself up to recently by its definition of literacy as merely the ability to read and write. The importance given to the formal linguistic aspects of texts, to the etymology of words and literal meanings, to correct grammar and accurate spelling, ensured attention to, and compliance with, the letter of the texts, but not necessarily with their spirit. Traditional academic practice, that emphasized form over meaning and had students interpret texts as if they were autonomous units, independent of a reader's response, implicitly imposed its own context of interpretation on all, claiming that its norms of interpretation were universal and accessible to anybody's intuition. Those students who were unable to interpret texts the way their teachers expected them to were called 'bad students', just as students may fail on National Standardized Academic Tests if they don't share the cultural norms of the National Educational Testing Services.

Social construction of literacy

Recent years have witnessed a rejection of what is now perceived to be an elitist and colonialist kind of literacy. The 'primitive' vs.

'civilized' dichotomy implied by the theory of the **Great Divide** between oral cultures (with little or no use of writing) and literate cultures (with a fuller utilization of writing and print), taken for granted until twenty years ago, is now put in question. Individual literacy has given way to the notion of multiple literacies as a plural set of social practices within social contexts of use. Thus, besides the traditional belletristic literacy, scholars now recognize other sorts of literacies linked to various genres (for example, literary literacy, press literacy, instructional manuals literacy, scientific literacy) that all have to do with the mastery of, or fluent control over, social uses of print language. In this regard, to be literate means not only to be able to encode and decode the written word, or to do exquisite text analyses; it is the capacity to understand and manipulate the social and cultural meanings of print language in thoughts, feelings, and actions.

Literacy, because it is not acquired naturally like orality, and is usually learned in schools, has long been confused with schooling. The cognitive skills claimed to devolve naturally from the ability to read and write have been shown to be due not to the written language *per se*, but to a distinct kind of schooling that prizes certain uses of language over others, whether it be spoken or written. The general educational value given to the ability to 'talk like a book'—i.e. to narrate events in clearly organized, analytical fashion, to construct an argument according to the logic of thesis–antithesis–synthesis, or problem–evidence–solution, to respond to 'what' and 'why' questions on texts, to convey information clearly and succinctly—stems from a belief that a context-reduced, topic-centered literacy is useful for all in all walks of life. Not everyone shares this belief, however; some argue that in occupations like the service or the marketing industries, or in the writing of novels or poems, other types of literacies are required, that schools traditionally do not impart. Furthermore, children from different social backgrounds bring to school different types of literacies, not all of which are validated by school literacy practices. For example, in the United States, children from African-American families might display a highly context-embedded, analogic, associative way of telling or writing stories that the school doesn't recognize as acceptable literate practice, whereas middle-class Anglos might have from home a more context-reduced, analytic, hierarchical narrative style that they find reinforced in the way schools teach texts.

If the acquisition of literacy is more than a matter of learning a new technology, but is indissociably linked to the values, social practices, and ways of knowing promoted in educational institutions, it may become the source of cultural conflict when the values of the school do not match those of the home. Such is the case in Alaska and Northern Canada, for example, where the Athabaskans' ways of learning and knowing are radically different from those of mainstream Anglo-Canadian and Anglo-American society. Even if they learn to read and write in English, Athabaskan children resist adopting Anglo-Saxon schooling practices that expect them, for example, to state their opinion about a text, take a point of view and defend it, display their abilities in front of others in the class, and speculate about future events—all verbal behaviors that are considered inappropriate in their own culture.

The two perspectives on literacy—literacy as mastery of the written medium, literacy as social practice—correspond to two different ways of viewing a stretch of written language: as text or as discourse. Each one has a different relation to the cultural context in which it is produced and received.

Text and discourse

The notion of **text** views a stretch of written language as the product of an identifiable authorial intention, and its relation to its context of culture as fixed and stable. Text meaning is seen as identical with the semantic signs it is composed of: text explication is used to retrieve the author's intended meaning, text deconstruction explores the associations evoked by the text. In both cases, however, neither what happens in the mind of the readers nor the social context of reception and production are taken into consideration. Such processes are the characteristics of **discourse**. A text cannot be given fuller meaning if it is not viewed also as discourse. To illustrate this, let us return to the Emily Dickinson poem of Chapter 1.

Essential Oils – are wrung –
The Attar from the Rose
Be not expressed by Suns – alone –
It is the gift of Screws –

The General Rose – decay –
But this – in Lady's Drawer
Make Summer – When the Lady lie
In Ceaseless Rosemary –

Like all other texts, this poem encodes cultural meaning through various cohesive devices that ensure logical and rhetorical continuity across sentences (see Chapter 2). For example, the deictic 'this' (The General Rose – decay – / But this – in Lady's Drawer) links 'the General Rose' and 'the Lady's Drawer', thus establishing a crucial cohesion between the two parts of the poem. But if we look more closely, 'this', followed by the silent dash and anchored in the perspective of the poet, seems to address the reader directly, by pointing to something outside the poem. Indeed, 'this' seems to refer to the poem itself, offered by the poet to the reader. The literate voice of the poem is here replaced by the orate engagement of the poem with the reader as a person. We can now view the deictic 'this' as either a demonstrative referring back to a prior element in the text (i.e. the antecedents 'Attar' or 'gift of Screws'), or as a new element pointing to the ongoing discourse between text and reader. In the first case, it is a cohesive device. In the second, it is a crucial factor of coherence.

As we saw in Chapter 2, cohesion brings cultural meaning into play within the text itself; coherence is established by the discourse it elicits between printed words and their readers. As in spoken exchanges (see Chapter 4), coherence is constructed by the reader who puts the signs on the page in relation to a variety of factors that can be found in the cultural context.

Coherence plays a particularly important role with poetic texts that are meant to engage the reader's emotions and sensibility, but it can also be found in other written texts. Take, for example, the label found on aspirin bottles:

> WARNING: Keep this and all medication out of the reach of children. As with any drug, if you are pregnant or nursing a baby, seek the advice of a health professional before using this

product. In the case of accidental overdosage, contact a physician or poison control center immediately.

This text is coherent, i.e. it makes sense for a reader who knows from prior personal or vicarious experience that drugs are bad both for children and for pregnant women, who understands the difference between a health professional and a physician, and who understands why you would go to the former if you are pregnant and to the latter if you had taken too much aspirin. In addition to prior experience, the reader makes sense of this text by associating it with other texts entitled 'WARNING', such as appear near electrical wires, places off limits and dangerous substances. However, prior experience and prior texts are not sufficient to render this text coherent. Why is it entitled 'WARNING' where the danger is not explicitly stated? Why should one go and seek help only in case of an 'accidental' overdose? Why does the text say 'overdosage' instead of 'overdose'? In order to make the text coherent, we have to draw on the two other contextual factors mentioned above; the text's purpose, and its conditions of production.

The pharmaceutical company that issued this warning wants to avoid lawsuits, but it also wants to avoid spreading panic among aspirin users, who might thereby refrain from buying the product. Thus it does not want to highlight the word 'dangerous' on its bottle, nor does it want to use the word 'overdose' because of its too close associations with the drug traffic scene. It wants to create the image of a reader as an intelligent mainstream person who could not possibly take an overdose of aspirin, unless by accident. The commercial and legal interests, i.e. the corporate culture, of the company have to be drawn into the interpretation of this text, in order to make it into a coherent discourse.

One of the greatest sources of difficulty for foreign readers is less the internal cohesion of the text than the cultural coherence of the discourse. For example, a sentence like 'Although he was over 20 years old, he still lived at home' written for an American readership, draws on the readers' cultural knowledge concerning young men's independence from their families, but might not be self-evident for readers from a culture where young men continue to live at home well into their twenties. Conversely, a sentence like

Ich habe Spaghetti gekocht, weil Kartoffeln heutzutage so teuer sind (I made spaghetti for dinner, because potatoes are so expensive nowadays), written for a German reader, draws on the cultural fact that many Germans always have potatoes with their meals; it may sound odd to an American reader with other culinary habits. The ability of the reader to interpret such logical connections shows how much coherence is dependent on the context of the literacy event itself.

Literacy event, prior text, point of view

The interaction of a reader, or community of readers, with texts of any kind has been called a **literacy event**. Literacy events are defined by their members' common social practices with written language (for instance, reading/writing/talking about family letters, attending/reciting religious services, attending/performing poetry readings, delivering/listening to scripted professional speeches, reading/writing scientific articles) and common ways of interpreting these practices.

The knowledge that goes into literacy events draws on the larger cultural and historical context of production and reception of texts in a particular discourse community. In the absence of the text's author and of its many other readers/interpreters, each reader has to reconstitute for herself her own understanding of the context, and thereby define her place *vis-à-vis* that context. This is similar to what happens in conversational exchanges of the kind we discussed at the beginning of Chapter 3. As with conversational contexts, the context for a literacy event includes a situational and a cultural dimension. The situational context includes:

1 The events captured in the propositional content.

2 The intended audience: what knowledge, values, interests, beliefs does the text assume it shares with its readers? How does the text position its audience, and position itself *vis-à-vis* its audience?

3 The text's purpose, i.e. the speech acts it contains: every sentence, as discussed in Chapters 2 and 3, both says something about the world (propositional or locutionary value), and

performs an action, for example, describe, inform, query, complain (illocutionary value). A text prompts its readers to ask themselves: Is this particular sentence a question? a statement? an order? a reproach? a criticism? an attack? In addition, every text attempts to have a cognitive and emotional effect on its readers, or to prompt its readers to action (perlocutionary value).

4 The text's register, or functional language variation according to the audience.

5 Its key: every text bears the mark of the narrator's stance—for example, ironic, humorous, or factual—*vis-à-vis* the facts related.

The context of a literacy event also includes a larger sociohistorical dimension which relates the text to other texts and to communal knowledge in general.

6 Prior texts: In the same manner as words refer to other words in the semantic world of signs (see Chapter 2), every text is a response to prior texts, prior language, prior issues raised through language. In order to understand a text, one has to understand what the text is responding to or against. This existing prior language, accumulated over the life of a discourse community, has been called **Discourse** with a capital D. Discourses, in this sense, are more than just language, they are ways of being in the world, or forms of life that integrate words, acts, values, beliefs, attitudes, and social identities. We return to this in the next chapter.

7 Point of view: One can distinguish three senses of the phrase point of view. The spatio-temporal point of view specifies the physical context that the narrator refers to. The psychological point of view has to do with the perspective adopted by the narrator, for example, that of an omniscient witness to the events narrated, or that of one of the characters in the story. The ideological point of view reveals the system of beliefs, values, and categories, by reference to which the narrator comprehends the world he/she refers to in the text. This last type of point of view is reflected in the metaphors that were mentioned in Chapter 2 (for instance, Argument is War) and by

which writers and readers understand persons and events. They generally index the type of discourse community the narrator belongs to.

Discourse communities, constituted, as we saw in Chapter 1, by common purposes, common interests, and beliefs, implicitly share a stock of prior texts and ideological points of view that have developed over time. These in turn encourage among their members common norms of interaction with, and interpretation of, texts that may be accepted or rejected by the members of these communities. The pressure to conform to these norms is exerted by the schools, the media, and by national and professional institutions. Thus the notion of literacy event leads inevitably to a consideration of the notion of genre.

Genre

Whereas a literacy event is defined as any interaction between readers and written texts within a social context, a **genre** is a socially sanctioned type of communicative event, either spoken—like a sermon, a joke, a lecture—or printed, like a press report, a novel, or a political manifesto. Although sometimes viewed as a universal type, fixed by literary and other conventions, a genre in a sociocultural perspective is always dependent on being perceived as such within a specific context of situation or culture.

The concept of genre is related to text type and language choice: it is as measured against a prototypical sermon in their culture, for example, that members of a group can assess to what extent the register chosen by a certain preacher conforms to or deviates from the genre 'sermon', even if it is not delivered in a church. As we saw in Chapter 4, misunderstandings can arise when some participants in a speech event believe they are engaged in one genre (for example, problem-solving task) while the other participants in the same event believe they are engaged in another (such as a talk show interview).

What turns a collection of communicative events into a genre is some conventionalized set of communicative purposes. For example, one convention of scientific research papers is that they inform researchers of scientists' findings as clearly, convincingly as possible, and in a manner that furthers future research. However, not every scientific community shares the same views as to how these goals should be achieved. There are striking differences, for example, between the French and the Anglo-Saxon genre 'research paper'. Anglo-Saxon scientists have to legitimize their research by displaying in the first paragraph all extant research on the same topic and showing how their own fills a neglected gap. By contrast, French scientific articles draw their legitimation from the status and affiliation of the researcher, and his/her own work in the field; French scientists find the initial review of the literature rather futile. Unlike their French counterparts, Anglo-Saxon scientists have to make explicit their adherence to a recognizable school, disciplinary tradition, or theoretical orientation; French scientists prefer their research to stand on its own merits. Whereas American research articles end with the obligatory discussion of 'the limitations of the study', French articles do no such thing; instead, they are obligated to raise larger questions, and point to directions for further areas of study. These two different styles within two scientific communities that otherwise share the same purpose may create difficulties for some French scientists, who may be willing to publish in English but wish to retain their own cultural scientific style.

It is easy to see why genre plays such a central role in the definition of culture. One can learn a lot about a discourse community's culture by looking at the names it gives to genres, for genre is society's way of defining and controlling meaning. In fact, the very definition of a text type as a separate genre, or a stylistic variation of the same genre, is a matter of passionate disputes, and not only among scholars. For, the concept of text type establishes constraints on what one is expected to write about, in what form, for what audience. Religious leaders in some cultures, like, for example, Shi'a Islam, make a difference between texts that tell the truth, for example, the sacred text of the Qur'an, and those that 'lie', such as poetry. Narrative irony, as found in the Western novel, is not a familiar text feature in a culture that expects narrative truth to be identical to real-life truth. Those who use novelistic irony and fiction to criticize Islamic practices, like Salman Rushdie did, are read at face-value and condemned by those who have the authority to be the textual gate-keepers of their culture.

Summary

The advent of writing and the invention of the printing press have radically changed the relation of language and culture. The maintenance of historical tradition, the control of collective memory, the authority to interpret events have all been enhanced by the written medium. Thus textual culture has become the dominant culture of research and scholarship.

However, there have always been two ways of looking at written language: as a fixed and stable product, i.e. as text, or as an interactive, highly inferential process between a text and its readers, i.e. as discourse. Through their educational system, their media, and their political institutions, discourse communities play an important role in establishing the parameters of socially acceptable literacy events, in defining the appropriate genres within their boundaries, and in seeing to it that these genres are respected by their members.

6

Language and cultural identity

In 1915, Edmond Laforest, a prominent Haitian writer, stood upon a bridge, tied a French Larousse dictionary around his neck, and leapt to his death. This symbolic, if fatal, grand gesture dramatizes the relation of language and cultural identity. Henry Louis Gates, who recounts this story, adds 'While other black writers, before and after Laforest, have been drowned artistically by the weight of various modern languages, Laforest chose to make his death an emblem of this relation of overwhelming indenture.' ('*Race', Writing, and Difference*. University of Chicago Press 1985, page 13). This event will help us bring together several notions that have emerged in the previous chapters; the motivated, non-arbitrary nature of the linguistic sign, the link between a language and its legitimate discourse community, the symbolic capital associated with the use of a particular language or of a literate form of that language, in short the association of language with a person's sense of self. We explore in this chapter the complex relationship between language and what is currently called 'cultural identity'.

Cultural identity

It is widely believed that there is a natural connection between the language spoken by members of a social group and that group's identity. By their accent, their vocabulary, their discourse patterns, speakers identify themselves and are identified as members of this or that speech and discourse community. From this membership, they draw personal strength and pride, as well as a sense of social importance and historical continuity from using the same language as the group they belong to.

But how to define which group one belongs to? In isolated, homogeneous communities like the Trobrianders studied by Malinowski, one may still define group membership according to common cultural practices and daily face-to-face interactions, but in modern, historically complex, open societies it is much more difficult to define the boundaries of any particular social group and the linguistic and **cultural identities** of its members.

Take ethnicity for example. In their 1982 survey conducted among the highly mixed population of Belize (formerly British Honduras), Le Page and Tabouret-Keller found out that different people ascribed themselves to different ethnicities as either 'Spanish', 'Creole', 'Maya' or 'Belizean', according to which ethnic criterion they focused on—physical features (hair and skin), general appearance, genetic descent, provenance, or nationality. Rarely was language used as an ethnically defining criterion. Interestingly, it was only under the threat of a Guatemalan takeover as soon as British rule would cease, that the sense of a Belizean national identity slowly started emerging from among the multiple ethnic ascriptions that people still give themselves to this day.

Group identity based on race would seem easier to define, and yet there are almost as many genetic differences, say, between members of the same White, or Black race as there are between the classically described human races, not to speak of the difficulty in some cases of ascertaining with 100 per cent exactitude a person's racial lineage. For example, in 1983 the South African Government changed the racial classification of 690 people: two-thirds of these, who had been Coloreds, became Whites, 71 who had been Blacks became Coloreds, and 11 Whites were redistributed among other racial groups! And, of course, there is no necessary correlation between a given racial characteristic and the use of a given language or variety of language.

Regional identity is equally contestable. As reported in the London *Times* of February 1984, when a Soviet book, *Populations of the World*, claimed that the population of France consisted of 'French, Alsatians, Flemings, Bretons, Basques, Catalans, Corsicans, Jews, Armenians, Gypsies and "others"',

Georges Marchais, the French Communist leader, violently disagreed: 'For us', he said, 'every man and woman of French nationality is French. France is not a multinational state: it is one nation, the product of a long history ....'

One would think that national identity is a clear-cut either/or affair (either you are or you are not a citizen), but it is one thing, for example, to have a Turkish passport, another thing to ascribe to yourself a Turkish national identity if you were born, raised and educated, say, in Germany, are a native speaker of German, and happen to have Turkish parents.

Despite the entrenched belief in the one language = one culture equation, individuals assume several collective identities that are likely not only to change over time in dialogue with others, but are liable to be in conflict with one another. For example, an immigrant's sense of self, that was linked in his country of origin perhaps to his social class, his political views, or his economic status, becomes, in the new country, overwhelmingly linked to his national citizenship or his religion, for this is the identity that is imposed on him by others, who see in him now, for example, only a Turk or a Muslim. His own sense of self, or cultural identity, changes accordingly. Out of nostalgia for the 'old country', he may tend to become more Turkish than the Turks and entertain what Benedict Anderson has called 'long distance nationalism'. The Turkish he speaks may become with the passing of years somewhat different from the Turkish spoken today in the streets of Ankara; the community he used to belong to is now more an 'imagined community' than the actual present-day Turkey.

Cultural stereotypes

The problem lies in equating the racial, ethnic, national identity imposed on an individual by the state's bureaucratic system, and that individual's self-ascription. Group identity is not a natural fact, but a cultural perception, to use the metaphor with which we started this book. Our perception of someone's social identity is very much culturally determined. What we perceive about a person's culture and language is what we have been conditioned by our own culture to see, and the stereotypical models already built around our own. Group identity is a question of **focusing** and

diffusion of ethnic, racial, national concepts or stereotypes. Let us take an example.

Le Page and Tabouret-Keller recount the case of a man in Singapore who claimed that he would never have any difficulty in telling the difference between an Indian and a Chinese. But how would he instantly know that the dark-skinned non-Malay person he saw on the street was an Indian (and not, say, a Pakistani), and that the light-skinned non-European was a Chinese (and not, say, a Korean), unless he differentiated the two according to the official Singaporean 'ethnic' categories: Chinese, Malay, Indian, Others? In another context with different racial classifications he might have interpreted differently the visual clues presented to him by people on the street. His impression was *focused* by the classificatory concepts prevalent in his society, a behavior that Benjamin Whorf would have predicted. In turn this focus may prompt him, by a phenomenon of *diffusion*, to identify all other 'Chinese' along the same ethnic categories, according to the stereotype 'All Chinese look alike to me'.

It has to be noted that societies impose racial and ethnic categories only on certain groups: Whites do not generally identify themselves by the color of their skin, but by their provenance or nationality. They would find it ludicrous to draw their sense of cultural identity from their membership in the White race. Hence the rather startled reaction of two Danish women in the United States to a young African-American boy, who, overhearing their conversation in Danish, asked them 'What's your culture?'. Seeing how perplexed they were, he explained with a smile 'See, I'm Black. That's my culture. What's yours?'. Laughingly they answered that they spoke Danish and came from Denmark. Interestingly, the boy did not use language as a criterion of group identity, but the Danes did.

European identities have traditionally been built much more around language and national citizenship, and around folk models of 'one nation = one language', than around ethnicity or race. But even in Europe the matter is not so simple. For example, Alsatians who speak German, French and Germanic Platt may alternatively consider themselves as primarily Alsatians, or French, or German, depending on how they position themselves *vis-à-vis* the history of their region and their family biography. A youngster born and raised in France of Algerian parents may, even though he speaks only French, call himself Algerian in France, but when abroad he might prefer to be seen as French, depending on which group he wishes to be identified with at the time.

Examples from other parts of the world show how complex the language–cultural identity relationship really is. The Chinese, for example, identify themselves ethnically as Chinese even though they speak languages or dialects which are mutually unintelligible. Despite the fact that a large number of Chinese don't know how to read and write, it is the Chinese character-writing system and the art of calligraphy that are the major factors of an overall Chinese group identity.

A further example of the difficulty of equating one language with one ethnic group is given by the case of the Sikhs in Britain. Threatened to lose public recognition of their cultural and religious distinctiveness, for example, the wearing of the Sikh turban in schools, Sikh religious leaders have tried to bolster the group's identity by promoting the teaching of Punjabi, endogamy, and patterns of behavior felt to be central to Sikhism, including hair styles and the wearing of turbans. However, seen objectively, neither the Punjabi language nor the wearing of turbans is peculiar to Sikhism either in India or Pakistan or Britain.

Many cultures have survived even though their language has virtually disappeared (for instance the Yiddish of Jewish culture, the Gullah of American Black culture, the Indian languages of East Indian culture in the Caribbean); others have survived because they were part of an oral tradition kept up within an isolated community (for example, Acadian French in Louisiana), or because their members learned the dominant language, a fact that ironically enabled them to keep their own. Thus in New Mexico, a certain Padre Martinez of Taos led the cultural resistance of Mexican Spanish speakers against the American occupation by encouraging them to learn English as a survival tool so that they could keep their Hispanic culture and the Spanish language alive.

Language crossing as act of identity

One way of surviving culturally in immigration settings is to exploit, rather than stifle, the endless variety of meanings afforded by participation in several discourse communities at once. More and more people are living, speaking and interacting in in-between spaces, across multiple languages or varieties of the same language: Latinos in Los Angeles, Pakistanis in London, Arabs in Paris, but also Black Americans in New York or Atlanta, choose one way of talking over another depending on the topic, the interlocutor and the situational context. Such **language crossings**, frequent in inter-ethnic communication, include, as we saw in Chapter 4, the switching of codes, i.e. the insertion of elements from one language into another, be they isolated words, whole sentences, or prosodic features of speech. Language crossing enables speakers to change footing within the same conversation, but also to show solidarity or distance towards the discourse communities whose languages they are using, and whom they perceive their interlocutor as belonging. By crossing languages, speakers perform cultural **acts of identity**. Thus, for example, two bilingual 12-year olds from Mexico in a US American school. M is telling F what she does when she comes back from school. M and F usually speak their common language, Spanish.

> M: Mira, me pongo a hacer tarea, después me pongo leer un libro, despues me pongo a hacer matemática, después de hacer matemática me pongo a practicar en el piano, después de terminarse en el piano=
>
> F: =you got a piano?
>
> M: I have a piano in my house, don't you guys know it? ... No me digas que no sabía ... yo lo dije a Gabriel y a Fernando ... todo el mundo.
>
> [M: Look, I do homework, then I read a book, then I do science, I do math, after doing math I practice the piano, after I finished with the piano =
>
> F: = you got a piano?
>
> M: I have a piano in my house, don't you guys know it? ... Don't tell me that you didn't know ... I told Gabriel and Fernando ... everybody]

(Unpublished data from Claire Kramsch)

The fact of owning a piano marks M as belonging to a different social culture than F who shows his surprise—and his distance—by using the dominant Anglo-American language. M acknowledges her membership in that culture by responding in English, but immediately switches back to Spanish to show her solidarity with her Latino peers in the classroom, who come from more modest backgrounds.

Refusing to adopt the same language when you are seen as belonging to the same culture can be perceived as an affront that requires some facework repair, as in the following radio interview between two Black American disk jockeys (DJ1, DJ2) and a Black American singer (SG):

DJ1: So whatz up wit da album shottie?
SG:　What's up with the album *shottie*
DJ1: Oh, excu:::se me. How are things progressing with your
　　　upcoming album?
(laughter)
　　　　Come on, girl! you know what I'm sayin'. You KNOW you
　　　　know da terminology! Don't front!
DJ2: Yeah, an' if ya don't know, now ya know
(laughter)
DJ1: Or at leas ack like ya know!
SG:　I know, I know, I'm jus' messin' wit y'all.
(Unpublished data from Claire Kramsch)

Language crossing can be used also for more complex stances by speakers who wish to display multiple cultural memberships and play off one against the other. Not infrequently speakers who belong to several cultures insert the intonation of one language into the prosody of another, or use phrases from one language as citational inserts into the other to distance themselves from alternative identities or to mock several cultural identities by stylizing, parodying, or stereotyping them all if it suits their social purposes of the moment. Thus, for example, the following stylization of Asian English or Creole English by Pakistani youngsters, native speakers of English, as a strategy to resist the authority of their Anglo teacher (BR) in a British school.

BR:　　attention gents
Asif:　yeh alright

Alan: alright

Asif: yeh

Kazim: (in Stylized Asian English) I AM VERY SORRY BEN JAAD

/aɪ æm veri sɒri ben ʤa:d/

Asif: (in Stylized Asian English) ATTENTION BENJAMIN

/əthenʃa:n benʤəmɪn/

...

BR: concentrate a little bit

...

Kazim: (in Creole English) stop moving **dat ting aroun**

/dæt tɪŋ əɪɑʊn/

(Rampton, Ben. *Crossing: Language and Ethnicity among Adolescents*. Longman 1995, pages 115–6.)

When speaking of cultural identity, then, we have to distinguish between the limited range of categories used by societies to classify their populations, and the identities that individuals ascribe to themselves under various circumstances and in the presence of various interlocutors. While the former are based on simplified and often quite stereotypical representations, the latter may vary with the social context. The ascription of cultural identity is particularly sensitive to the perception and acceptance of an individual by others, but also to the perception that others have of themselves, and to the distribution of legitimate roles and rights that both parties hold within the discourse community. Cultural identity, as the example of Edmond Laforest shows, is a question of both indenture to a language spoken or imposed by others, and personal, emotional investment in that language through the apprenticeship that went into acquiring it. The dialectic of the individual and the group can acquire dramatic proportions when nationalistic language policies come into play.

Linguistic nationism

The association of one language variety with the membership in one national community has been referred to as **linguistic nationism**. For example, during the French Revolution, the concept of a national language linked to a national culture was intended to systematically replace the variety of regional dialects and local practices. Between 1790 and 1792 a questionnaire was sent by l'Abbé Grégoire to lawyers, clergymen, and politicians in the French provinces under the pretext of documenting and cataloguing the linguistic and ethnographic uses of the thirty local 'patois' spoken in France at the time. In fact, through this survey, the Jacobins established a blueprint for the subsequent systematic eradication of these patois. Historians have debated whether the conscious governmental policy of annihilation of local dialects in France at the time was done for the sake of national or ideological unity, or in order to establish the dominance of bourgeois Parisian culture over the uncouth peasant culture, or in order to break the strong cultural monopoly of the Catholic Church who catechized its faithful in the local vernaculars. Linguistic wars are always also political and cultural wars. Efforts by present-day France to cultivate a network of French speakers around the world, and link it to a francophone identity, or *francophonie*, must be seen as a way of countering the overwhelming spread of English by offering speakers a supranational cultural identity that is exclusively linguistic. French as an international language remains monitored by the Académie Française, a French national institution that is seen as the guarantor of cultural purity—in the same manner as English as an international language is monitored in scientific circles by Anglo-American journals who serve as the gate-keepers of a certain intellectual style of scientific research (see Chapter 5).

As we saw in Chapter 1, it has been argued that the modern nation is an imagined community that originated in eighteenth century bourgeois imagination, and has relied heavily on print capitalism for its expression and dissemination. The modern nation is imagined as limited by finite, if elastic boundaries; it is imagined as a sovereign state, but also as a fraternal community of comrades, ready to take arms to defend their territorial integrity or their economic interests. This prototype of the modern nation as a cultural entity is, of course, a utopia. It has been mirrored by a similar view of language as shared patrimony, a self-contained, autonomous, and homogeneous linguistic system based on a homogeneous social world—in other words, a linguistic utopia. Such imaginings are tenacious and contribute to what we call an individual's national 'identity'.

When new nation-states emerge, such as more recently Belize, the mere category of national identity may, as a side effect, put a stress on other categories such as Spanishness or Mayaness, that in turn may acquire renewed importance, since the Spanish population and the Maya population do not coincide with the borders of Belize, but go beyond them to form new supranational alliances. This is what has happened in Europe with the Basque and Catalan identities that cross, linguistically and culturally, the national borders of France and Spain, and thus replace the nation by the region, and the national language by the regional language as units of cultural identification.

Nation-states respond to such separatist tendencies by refocusing national identity either around a national language or around the concept of multiculturalism. Current efforts by the US English Movement in the United States to amend the Constitution by declaring English the official national language have to be seen as the attempt to ensure not only mutual linguistic intelligibility, but cultural homogeneity as well. In periods of social fragmentation and multiple identities, each clamoring to be recognized, language takes on not only an indexical, but a symbolic value, according to the motto 'Let me hear you speak and I will tell you who you *are loyal to*'. The link between the US English legislation and anti-immigration legislation has been frequently pointed out by critics.

Besides being used as a means of excluding outsiders, as we saw in Chapter 1, the use of one, and only one, language is often perceived as a sign of political allegiance. The remark 'I had ten years of French and I still can't …' may be the expression not so much of bilingual failure as of monolingual pride. People who, by choice or by necessity, have traditionally been bi- or multilingual, like migrants and cosmopolitans, have often been held in suspicion by those who ascribe to themselves a monovocal, stable, national identity.

Standard language, cultural totem

The way this national identity is expressed is through an artificially created **standard language**, fashioned from a multiplicity of dialects. When one variety of a language is selected as an indicator of difference between insiders and outsiders, it can be shielded from variations through official grammars and dictionaries and can be taught through the national educational system. For example, in the times of the Ancient Greeks, any person whose language was not Greek was called a 'barbarian', i.e. an alien from an inferior culture. Hence the term **barbarism** to denote any use of language that offends contemporary standards of correctness or purity. In some countries that have a National Academy for the preservation of the national linguistic treasure against external imports and internal degradation, misuses of the standard language by its speakers are perceived not only as linguistic mishaps, but as aesthetic and moral offences as well (hence derogatory verbs like 'butchering' or 'slaughtering' a language).

Note that standard language is always a written form of the language, preserved, as we saw in the last chapter, through a distinct print culture serving a variety of political, economic, and ideological interests. But it is well known that even though educated people will display strong views about what 'good' language use is supposed to be like, when they speak they often themselves commit precisely those barbarisms they so strongly condemn. The desire to halt the march of time and keep language pure of any cultural contamination is constantly thwarted by the co-construction of culture in every dialogic encounter (see Chapter 3).

Language acquires a symbolic value beyond its pragmatic use and becomes a totem of a cultural group, whenever one dialect variety is imposed on others in the exercise of national or colonial power (France), or when one language is imposed over others through the deliberate, centralized pressure of a melting pot ideology (English over French in Louisiana, English over Spanish in New Mexico), or when one language supplants others through centralized deliberate planning or diffuse societal forces (the spread of English as an international language). The totemization of the dominant language leads to the stigmatization of the dominated languages.

Members of a group who feel that their cultural and political identity is threatened are likely to attach particular importance to the maintenance or resurrection of 'their language' (for example, Quebec, Belgium, Wales among many others). The particularly poignant death of Edmond Laforest is a reminder of the deeply personal association of language with one's self-ascribed cultural identity, especially when the recognition of that linguistic identity is denied. Laforest's despair was compounded by the intransigently literate view that the majority of educated French (or those who want to be seen as educated) hold toward their national language. By having learned and adopted the literate idiom of the colonial occupant, the Haitian poet may have felt he had betrayed not only his Haitian Creole identity, but also the rich oral tradition of his ancestors.

Linguistic and cultural imperialism

Laforest's death in 1915 acquired a new meaning when recounted in 1985, at a time when linguistic rights were starting to be viewed as basic human rights. The case for **linguistic rights** has been made particularly strongly with regard to the hegemonic spread of English around the world. Beyond the symbolic link frequently established between language and territorial or cultural identity, there is also another link that has more to do with the promulgation of global ideologies through the worldwide expansion of one language, also called **linguicism**. Linguicism has been defined as 'ideologies, structures, and practices which are used to legitimate, effectuate, and reproduce an unequal division of power and resources (both material and unmaterial) between groups which are defined on the basis of language', as Phillipson says in his book *Linguistic Imperialism* (Oxford University Press 1992, page 47), in which English **linguistic imperialism** is seen as a type of linguicism.

From our discussion so far, one can see where the self-ascription to a given group on the basis of language might be the response to rather than the cause of the lack of material and spiritual power. It is when people feel economically and ideologically disempowered that language may become an issue and a major symbol of cultural integrity. However, as we saw in Chapters 2 and 3, in a world of signs where every meaning can proliferate *ad infinitum*, it becomes very difficult to distinguish what is the effect and what is the cause of linguistic imperialism. The spread of English is undeniable, and it is viewed by those who suffer from it as a totem for a certain Anglo-American 'culture' or way of life, but it is not clear whether the appropriate response in the long run is to make English and other languages into cultural icons, or to rely on the remarkable ability that speakers have to create multiple cultural realities in any language.

This is not to say that linguistic pluralism is not a desirable good in itself. The Babel threat is not the splintering off in mutually unintelligible languages, but the monopoly of one language over others. As in Babel's days, the complacent belief that people are working for a common cause just because they speak a common language is a dangerous illusion. Being human means working through the shoals of mutual misunderstandings across incommensurable languages. That is why linguistic rights, like anti-trust laws, have to be upheld, not because of the one-to-one relationship between culture and language, but because each language provides a uniquely communal, and uniquely individual, means by which human beings apprehend the world and one another.

Summary

Although there is no one-to-one relationship between anyone's language and his or her cultural identity, language is *the* most sensitive indicator of the relationship between an individual and a given social group. Any harmony or disharmony between the two is registered on this most sensitive of the Richter scales. Language is an integral part of ourselves—it permeates our very thinking and way of viewing the world. It is also the arena where political and cultural allegiances and loyalties are fought out. However, if language indexes our relation to the world, it is not itself this relation.

Because of the inevitable and necessary indeterminacy of signs, the same use of a given language can index both indenture and investment, both servitude and emancipation, both powerlessness and empowerment. Paradoxically, the only way to preserve the room for maneuver vital to any human communication is not by making sure that everyone speaks the same language, but by making sure that the linguistic semiotic capital of humankind remains as rich and as diversified as possible.

7
Current issues

The relationship of language and culture in language study is one of the most hotly debated issues at the present time. Because language is closely related to the way we think, and to the way we behave and influence the behavior of others, the notion that our sense of social reality may be but a construction of language or 'language game' is disturbing. The notion that a person's social and cultural identity may not be the immutable monolithic entity it is usually taken for, but a kaleidoscope of various presentations and representations of self through language, is unsettling. These uncertainties explain in part the current debates surrounding the role of the native speaker, the concept of cultural authenticity, the notions of cross-, inter-, and multicultural communication and what has become known as **the politics of recognition** (see page 124).

Who is a native speaker?

Linguists have relied on **native speakers**' natural intuitions of grammatical accuracy and their sure sense of what is proper language use to establish a norm against which the performance of non-native speakers is measured. Native speakers have traditionally enjoyed a natural prestige as language teachers, because they are seen as not only embodying the 'authentic' use of the language, but as representing its original cultural context as well. In recent times, the identity as well as the authority of the native speaker have been put into question. The 'native speaker' of linguists and language teachers is in fact an abstraction based on arbitrarily selected features of pronunciation, grammar and lexicon, as well as on stereotypical features of appearance and demeanor. For example, children of Turkish parents and bearing a Turkish surname, but born, raised, and educated in Germany may have some difficulty being perceived as native speakers of German when applying for a language teaching job abroad, so entrenched is the association of one language with one national stereotype in the public imagination, as discussed in the last chapter. The native speaker is, moreover, a monolingual, mono-cultural abstraction; he/she is one who speaks only his/her (standardized) native tongue and lives by one (standardized) national culture. In reality, most people partake of various languages or language varieties and live by various cultures and subcultures (see Chapter 1).

Hence, we are faced once again with the old nature/culture debate. It is not clear whether one is a native speaker by birth, or by education, or by virtue of being recognized and accepted as a member of a like-minded cultural group. If the last seems to be the case, ideal nativeness and claims to a certain ownership of a language must give way to multifarious combinations of language use and membership in various discourse communities—more than has been up to now assumed under the label 'native speaker'.

Cultural authenticity

Much of the discussion surrounding the native speaker has been focused around two concepts: authenticity and **appropriateness**. By analogy with the creation of standard languages, nation-states have promoted a standardized notion of cultural authenticity that has served to rally emotional identification both at home and abroad. Stereotypes, like French chic, German know-how, American casualness, are shorthand symbols, readily recognized and applied to their respective realities; they help draw cultural boundaries between Us and Others in order to appreciate the uniqueness of both. Language learners, keen on slipping into someone else's shoes by learning their language, attach great importance to the cultural authenticity of French bread or German train schedules, and the cultural appropriateness of Japanese salutations or Chinese greeting ceremonies. Their desire to learn the language of others is often coupled with a desire to behave and think like them, in order to ultimately be recognized and validated by them.

However, two factors are putting the notion of authenticity and appropriateness in language learning into question. First, the diversity of authenticities within one national society, depending on such contextual variables as age, social status, gender, ethnicity, race; what is authentic in one context might be inauthentic in another. Second, the undesirability of imposing on learners a concept of authenticity that might devalue their own authentic selves *as learners*. Thus cultural appropriateness may need to be replaced by the concept of **appropriation**, whereby learners make a foreign language and culture their own by adopting and adapting it to their own needs and interests. The ability to acquire another person's language and understand someone else's culture while retaining one's own is one aspect of a more general ability to mediate between several languages and cultures, called cross-cultural, intercultural, or multicultural communication.

Cross-cultural, intercultural, multicultural

Depending on how culture is defined and which discipline one comes from, various terms are used to refer to communication between people who don't share the same nationality, social or ethnic origin, gender, age, occupation, or sexual preference. The nomenclature overlaps somewhat in its use.

The term 'cross-cultural' or **intercultural** usually refers to the meeting of two cultures or two languages across the political boundaries of nation-states. They are predicated on the equivalence of one nation–one culture–one language, and on the expectation that a 'culture shock' may take place upon crossing national boundaries. In foreign language teaching a cross-cultural approach seeks ways to understand the Other on the other side of the border by learning his/her national language.

The term intercultural may also refer to communication between people from different ethnic, social, gendered cultures within the boundaries of the same national language. Both terms are used to characterize communication, say, between Chinese-Americans and African-Americans, between working-class and upper-class people, between gays and heterosexuals, between men and women. Intercultural communication refers to the dialogue between minority cultures and dominant cultures, and are associated with issues of bilingualism and biculturalism.

The term **multicultural** is more frequently used in two ways. In a societal sense, it indicates the coexistence of people from many different backgrounds and ethnicities, as in 'multicultural societies'. In an individual sense, it characterizes persons who belong to various discourse communities, and who therefore have the linguistic resources and social strategies to affiliate and identify with many different cultures and ways of using language. The cultural identity of multicultural individuals is not that of multiple native speakers, but, rather, it is made of a multiplicity of social roles or 'subject positions' which they occupy selectively, depending on the interactional context in which they find themselves at the time.

The politics of recognition

Finally we turn to the difficult and complex issue of what has been called 'tolerance', 'empathy', or, from a political perspective, 'recognition' of other cultures. Individuals need to be recognized both in their individual and in their social group identity. But as with facework (see Chapter 4), these two demands might be incompatible. As individuals, they deserve the same respect and human rights protection given to all individuals by the laws of a democratic society; but as members of a cultural group they deserve to be given special rights and recognition. In other words, 'I want you to recognize me as the same as you, but at the same time I want you to recognize how different I am from you'. Simply put: should one recognize sameness or separateness?

The struggle for recognition, expressed here as 'we are equal but different', seems to be based on an assumption of equal worth, where 'I' or 'you' can be 'we' because we share a tight common purpose and can work towards the common good. But a common purpose and a common definition of what is good precludes any differentiation of roles and world views. Both the universal and the particular are abstractions that gloss over more fundamental realities of unequal power, authority, and legitimation. What is needed, then, is not peremptory and inauthentic judgments of equal value or of the relative worth of different cultures, but a willingness to accept that our horizons might be displaced as we attempt to understand the other. In the same manner as we should not confuse bureaucratic and self-ascribed cultural identity, so we should not presume that the cultural categories we use to judge the worth of other cultures are universal.

Given the recent large-scale migrations around the world, this is a difficult issue that politicians are grappling with in almost every industrialized society. National governments that promote multicultural, multiracial harmony like Singapore or the US, one could argue, in fact enhance ethnic separateness by constantly drawing attention to 'racial' and 'ethnic' identities. Such distinctions may be bolstered by religion. For example, in Singapore, the differing beliefs and practices of Chinese Taoists or Buddhists, Indian Hindus, Muslims or Sikhs, and Islamic Malays maintain cultural and ethnic separatism despite the strong claim to a national Singaporean identity. These distinctions might also be strengthened by the educational system, for instance in the United States where a decentralized school system, financed mainly by local property taxes, ensures the perpetuation in schools of the local social class structure and local ethnic and racial distribution.

In modern urban communities where the individual cannot rely on predefined social scripts, nor on universally or nationally accepted moral principles, to find his/her cultural self, cultural identities are seen as being formed in open dialogue with others. Communicative practices reflect institutionalized networks of relationships, defined by the family, the school, the workplace, the professional organization, the church, each with its own power hierarchy, its expected roles and statuses, its characteristic values and beliefs, attitudes and ideologies. This may be as far as we may go in defining the boundaries of one's cultural identity. Geographic mobility, professional change, and the vagaries of life may give a person multiple social identities that all get played out alternately on the complex framings and reframings of daily encounters.

However, such a multicultural view of the link between language and cultural identity has to be recognized as stemming, itself, from an urban, industrialized intellectual tradition. A growing gulf is opening up not between national cultures, but between those who can afford to be supranational cosmopolitans—through access to the Internet, travel privileges, knowledge of several languages beside English, ability and freedom to code-switch between them—and those who are rooted in one national or religious culture. The description suggested above of the plurality and multiplicity of cultural identities within one individual might be violently rejected by people from a different intellectual tradition for whom categories of identity are much more stable consensual affairs.

This brief survey of the multifarious links between language and culture has led us from a study of signs and their meanings all the way to issues of cultural identity and cultural survival. In the realm of the symbolic, the stakes are high. Equally urgent is the necessity to cast as broad a semiotic net as possible in the study of language and culture, and to honor the marvelous difference and diversity among and within human beings.

Readings

Chapter 1
The relationship of language and culture

Text 1

EDWARD SAPIR: *Selected Writings of Edward Sapir in Language, Culture, and Personality*. Edited by David G. Mandelbaum. University of California Press 1949, page 162.

This well-known statement from linguist and anthropologist Edward Sapir grew out of his studies of American Indian languages. In this passage, Sapir lays the ground for the principle of linguistic relativity.

Language is a guide to 'social reality'. Though language is not ordinarily thought of as of essential interest to the students of social science, it powerfully conditions all our thinking about social problems and processes. Human beings do not live in the objective world alone, nor alone in the world of social activity as ordinarily understood, but are very much at the mercy of the particular language which has become the medium of expression for their society. It is quite an illusion to imagine that one adjusts to reality essentially without the use of language and that language is merely an incidental means of solving specific problems of communication or reflection. The fact of the matter is that the 'real world' is to a large extent unconsciously built up on the language habits of the group. No two languages are ever sufficiently similar to be considered as representing the same social reality. The worlds in which different societies live are distinct worlds, not merely the same world with different labels attached ... We see and hear and otherwise experience very largely as we do because the language habits of our community predispose certain choices of interpretation.

▷ *Why do you think Sapir distinguishes between 'distinct worlds' and 'the same world with different labels attached'?*

▷ *Is Sapir claiming here that our language* determines *the way we think?*

Text 2
BENJAMIN LEE WHORF: *Language, Thought and Reality: Selected Writings of Benjamin Lee Whorf.* Edited by John B. Carroll. Massachusetts Institute of Technology Press 1956, pages 212, 213, 221.

The following passages are the most cited and the most controversial of Whorf's statements on linguistic relativity. We recognize here some of his main themes: language and thought reinforce each other; language not only reflects, but also shapes reality; grammar is not universal, it is particular to each language.

[T]he background linguistic system (in other words, the grammar) of each language is not merely a reproducing instrument for voicing ideas but rather is itself the shaper of ideas, the program and guide for the individual's mental activity, for his analysis of impressions, for his synthesis of his mental stock in trade. Formulation of ideas is not an independent process, strictly rational in the old sense, but is part of a particular grammar, and differs, from slightly to greatly, between different grammars. We dissect nature along lines laid down by our native languages. The categories and types that we isolate from the world of phenomena we do not find there because they stare every observer in the face; on the contrary, the world is presented in a kaleidoscopic flux of impressions which has to be organized by our minds—and this means largely by the linguistic systems in our minds. We cut nature up, organize it into concepts, and ascribe significances as we do, largely because we are parties to an agreement to organize it in this way—an agreement that holds throughout our speech community and is codified in the patterns of our language. The agreement is, of course, an implicit and unstated one, *but its terms*

terms are absolutely obligatory; we cannot talk at all except by subscribing to the organization and classification of data which the agreement decrees ... .

From this fact proceeds what I have called the 'linguistic relativity principle', which means, in informal terms, that users of markedly different grammars are pointed by their grammars toward different types of observations and different evaluations of externally similar acts of observation, and hence are not equivalent as observers, but must arrive at somewhat different views of the world.

▷ *What does Whorf mean by the phrase 'mental stock in trade'?*

▷ *The phrase in italics is the one that earned Whorf the most criticism. Can you imagine why?*

▷ *While Sapir saw ideas as shaped by the 'language habits of the group' (see Text 1), Whorf sees them as shaped by the 'grammar' itself. Do you see a potential difference there between Sapir's and Whorf's views on linguistic relativity?*

▷ *Show with a concrete example how a grammatical feature in one language formulates an idea which cannot be easily expressed through the grammar of another language.*

Text 3

STEVEN PINKER: *The Language Instinct.* Harper 1995, pages 60 and 61.

▷ *As a cognitive scientist, Steven Pinker uses psychological arguments to shoot down Whorf's claim about the relationship of language and thought.*

What led Whorf to this radical position? He wrote that the idea first occurred to him in his work as a fire prevention engineer when he was struck by how language led workers to misconstrue dangerous situations. For example, one worker caused a serious explosion by tossing a cigarette into an 'empty' drum that in fact was full of gasoline vapor. Another lit a blowtorch near a 'pool of water' that was really a basin of decomposing tannery waste, which, far from being 'watery,' was releasing inflammable gases. Whorf's studies of American languages strengthened his conviction. For example, in Apache, *It is a dripping spring* must be expressed 'As water, or springs, whiteness moves downward.' 'How utterly unlike our way of thinking!', he wrote.

But the more you examine Whorf's arguments, the less sense they make. Take the story about the worker and the 'empty' drum. The seeds of disaster supposedly lay in the semantics of *empty*, which, Whorf claimed, means both 'without its usual contents' and 'null and void, empty, inert.' The hapless worker, his conception of reality molded by his linguistic categories, did not distinguish between the 'drained' and 'inert' senses, hence, flick … boom! But wait. Gasoline vapor is invisible. A drum with nothing but vapor in it looks just like a drum with nothing in it at all. Surely this walking catastrophe was fooled by his eyes, not by the English language.

The example of whiteness moving downward is supposed to show that the Apache mind does not cut up events into distinct objects and actions. Whorf presented many such examples from Native American languages. The Apache equivalent of *The boat is grounded on the beach* is 'It is on the beach pointwise as an event of canoe motion.' *He invites people to a feast* becomes 'He, or somebody, goes for eaters of cooked food.' … All this, to be sure, is utterly unlike our way of talking. But do we know that it is utterly unlike our way of thinking?

As soon as Whorf's articles appeared, the psycholinguists Eric Lenneberg and Roger Brown pointed out two non sequiturs in his argument. First Whorf did not actually study any Apaches, it is not clear that he ever met one. His assertions about Apache psychology are based entirely on Apache grammar—making his argument circular. Apaches speak differently, so they must think differently. How do we know that they think differently? Just listen to the way they speak!

Second, Whorf rendered the sentences as clumsy, word-for-word translations, designed to make the literal meanings seem as odd as possible. But looking at the actual glosses that Whorf provided, I could, with equal grammatical justification, render the first sentence as the mundane 'Clear stuff—water—is falling.' Turning the tables, I could take the English sentence 'He walks' and render it 'As solitary masculinity, leggedness proceeds.'

▷ In the first two paragraphs, Pinker seems to claim that people are guided by their senses more than by the language that surrounds them. Do you agree?

▷ Pinker pushes Whorf's claims ad absurdum. How would you respond to each of these two arguments?

Text 4

JOHN J. GUMPERZ AND STEPHEN C. LEVINSON:
'Introduction: linguistic relativity re-examined' in J. J. Gumperz and S. C. Levinson (Eds.): *Rethinking Linguistic Relativity*.
Cambridge University Press 1996, page 1.

In the late 1990s, linguists and anthropologists revisited the notion of linguistic relativity in light of developments in cognitive science, ethnography, and the sociology of language. Taking an anthropological and a pragmatic perspective respectively, Gumperz and Levinson propose a balanced view that acknowledges the universal aspects of language as well as its particular manifestations in individual speakers in varied contexts of use.

Every student of language or society should be familiar with the essential idea of linguistic relativity, the idea that culture, *through* language, affects the way we think, especially perhaps our classification of the experienced world. Much of our experience seems to support some such idea, for example the phenomenology of struggling with a second language, where we find that the summit of competence is forever over the next horizon, the obvious absence of definitive or even accurate translation (let alone the ludicrous failure of phrasebooks), even the wreck of diplomatic efforts on linguistic and rhetorical rocks.

On the other hand, there is a strand of robust common sense that insists that a stone is a stone whatever you call it, that the world is a recalcitrant reality that imposes its structure on our thinking and our speaking and that the veil of linguistic difference can be ripped aside with relative ease. Plenty of subjective experiences and objective facts can be marshalled to support this view: the delight of foreign friendships, our ability to 'read' the military or economic strategies of alien rivals, the very existence of comparative sciences of language, psychology, and society.

> Explain what Gumperz and Levinson mean in this context by the phrase 'the phenomenology of struggling with a second language', and how that would support the principle of linguistic relativity.

> Give further 'subjective experiences and objective facts' that might contest the validity of linguistic relativity.

Chapter 2
Meaning as sign

Text 5

EDWARD SAPIR: *Selected Writings of Edward Sapir in Language, Culture, and Personality.* Edited by David G. Mandelbaum. University of California Press 1949, pages 157–9.

According to the principle of linguistic relativity, culture is encoded in the lexicon and the syntax of a language and the following examples illustrate this. We have to ask ourselves, however, if the very description in English *of linguistic phenomena experienced by speakers of other languages* in their respective languages *can ever correspond to their own experience of their language. Linguistic relativity applies also to the description of linguistic phenomena.*

[W]hen we observe an object of the type that we call a 'stone' moving through space towards the earth, we involuntarily analyze the phenomenon into two concrete notions, that of a stone and that of an act of falling, and, relating these two notions to each other by certain formal methods proper to English, we declare that 'the stone falls.' We assume, naively enough, that this is about the only analysis that can properly be made. And yet, if we look into the way that other languages take to express this very simple kind of impression, we soon realize how much may be added to, subtracted from, or rearranged in our own form of expression without materially altering our report of the physical fact.

In German and in French, we are compelled to assign 'stone' to a gender category; ... in Chippewa we cannot express ourselves without bringing in the apparently irrelevant fact that a stone is an inanimate object. If we find gender beside the point, the Russians may wonder why we consider it necessary to specify in every case whether a stone, or any other object for that matter, is conceived in a definite or an indefinite manner, why the difference between 'the stone' and 'a stone' matters. 'Stone falls' is good enough for Lenin, as it was good enough for Cicero ... The Kwakiutl Indian of British Columbia may ... wonder why we do not go a step further and indicate in some way whether the stone is visible or invisible to the speaker at the moment of speaking and whether it is nearest to the speaker, the person addressed, or some third party ... We insist on expressing the singularity of the falling object, where the Kwakiutl Indian, differing from the Chippewa, can generalize and make a statement which would apply equally well to one or several stones. Moreover, he need not specify the time of the fall. The Chinese get on with a minimum of explicit formal statement and content themselves with a frugal 'stone fall.' ... In the Nootka language the combined impression of a stone falling is quite differently analyzed. The stone need not be specifically referred to, but a single word, a verb form, may be used ... 'it stones down'.

▷ *How far is Sapir's view here consistent with the remark in Text 4 that 'there is a strand of common sense that insists that a stone is a stone whatever you call it'? How common is common sense?*

▷ *What cultural meanings might be expressed by each of these different encodings of the stone-falling event?*

Text 6

GEORGE LAKOFF and MARK JOHNSON: *Metaphors we Live By*. University of Chicago Press 1980, pages 3–5.

Culture is encoded not only in the semantic structures of a language, but also in its idiomatic expressions that both reflect and direct the way we think. Different languages predispose their speakers to view reality in different ways through the different metaphors they use.

In most of the little things we do every day, we simply think and act more or less automatically along certain lines. Just what these lines are is by no means obvious. One way to find out is by looking at language ... Primarily on the basis of linguistic evidence, we have found that most of our ordinary conceptual system is metaphorical in nature ...

To give some idea of what it could mean for a concept to be metaphorical and for such a concept to structure an everyday activity, let us start with the concept ARGUMENT and the conceptual metaphor ARGUMENT IS WAR. This metaphor is reflected in our everyday language by a wide variety of expressions:

> ARGUMENT IS WAR
> Your claims are *indefensible*
> He *attacked every weak point* in my argument
> His criticisms were *right on target*
> I *demolished* his argument
> I've never *won* an argument with him
> You disagree? Okay, *shoot*!
> If you use that strategy, he'll *wipe you out*
> He *shot down* all of my arguments

It is important to see that we don't just *talk* about arguments in terms of war. We can actually win or lose arguments. We see the person we are arguing with as an opponent. We attack his positions and we defend our own ... Many of the things we *do* in arguing are partially structured by the concept of war. Though there is no physical battle, there is a verbal battle ... It is in this sense that the ARGUMENT IS WAR metaphor is one that we live by in this culture; it structures the actions we perform in arguing.

Try to imagine a culture where arguments are not viewed in terms of war, where no one wins or loses, where there is no sense of attacking or defending, gaining or losing ground. Imagine a culture where an argument is viewed as a dance, the participants are seen as performers, and the goal is to perform in a balanced and aesthetically pleasing way. In such a culture, people would view arguments differently, experience them differently, carry them out differently, and talk about them differently. But *we* would probably not view them as arguing at all: they would simply be doing something different. It would seem strange even to call what they were doing 'arguing'.

▷ Do you think the examples given in Text 6 above could be interpreted differently than 'Argument is war'? And if so, what does that say about linguistic relativity?

▷ Can you think of a few metaphors that members of the culture mentioned in the last paragraph of this passage might use when referring to 'arguments'?

▷ Does Lakoff and Johnson's example mean that members of this fictitious culture never argue?

Text 7

ANNA WIERZBICKA: *Semantics, Culture, and Cognition.* Oxford University Press 1992, page 119.

In the search for a universal base from which various linguistic encodings could be compared across cultures (like, for Sapir, the universal perception of a 'stone falling'), linguists have often used human emotions, in the belief that emotions are universally human. Recently, this universality has been put into question.

Are emotions universal or culture-specific?

According to Izard and Buechler (1980:168), the fundamental emotions are (1) interest, (2) joy, (3) surprise, (4) sadness, (5) anger, (6) disgust, (7) contempt, (8) fear, (9) shame/shyness, and (10) guilt …. I view [this] claim with skepticism. If lists such as the preceding are supposed to enumerate universal human emotions, how is it that these emotions are all so neatly identified by means of English words? For example, Polish does not have a word corresponding exactly to the English word *disgust*. What if the psychologists working on the 'fundamental human emotions' happened to be native speakers of Polish rather than English? Would it still have occurred to them to include 'disgust' on their list? An Australian Aboriginal language, Gidjingali, does not lexically distinguish 'fear' from 'shame', subsuming feelings kindred to those identified by the English words *fear* and *shame* under one lexical item …. If the researchers happened to be native speakers of Gidjingali rather than English, would it still have occurred to them to claim that fear and shame are both fundamental human emotions, discrete and clearly separated from each other?

English terms of emotion constitute a folk taxonomy, not an objective, culture-free analytical framework, so obviously we cannot assume that English words such as *disgust, fear,* or *shame* are clues to universal human concepts or to basic psychological realities. Yet words such as these are usually treated as if they were objective, culture-free 'natural kinds'.

▷ *Ask a bilingual person what he/she associates with words like English 'disgust' and its counterpart in her other language. Elicit her associations first in English, then in the other language. Compare the two sets of associations.*

Chapter 3
Meaning as action

Text 8

BRONISLAW MALINOWSKI: 'The Problem of Meaning in Primitive Languages' in C.K. Ogden and I.A. Richards (Eds): *The Meaning of Meaning.* Harcourt Brace 1923, pages 457–8.

In this text, we see an anthropologist at work, trying to make sense of the signs that surround him. Malinowski's ethnographies of the Trobriand Islanders have inspired generations of anthropologists, like Clifford Geertz (Text 10).

Imagine yourself suddenly transported onto a coral atoll in the Pacific, sitting in a circle of natives and listening to their conversation. Let us assume further that there is an ideal interpreter at hand, who, as far as possible, can convey the meaning of each utterance, word for word, so that the listener is in possession of all the linguistic data available. Would that make you understand the conversation or even a single utterance? Certainly not.

Let us look at such a text, an actual utterance taken down from a conversation of natives in the Trobriand Islands, N. E. New Guinea ...

Tasakaulo	kaymatana	yakida;	
We run	front-wood	ourselves;	

tawoulo	oranu;	tasivila	tagine
we paddle	in place;	we turn	we see

soda;		isakaulo	ka'u'uya
companion ours;		he runs	rear-wood

oluvieki	similaveta	Pilolu
behind	their sea-arm	Pilolu

The verbatim English translation of this utterance sounds at first like a riddle or a meaningless jumble of words; certainly not like a significant, unambiguous statement. Now if the listener ... were to understand even the general trend of this statement, he would have first to be informed about the situation in which these words were spoken. He would need to have them placed in their proper setting of native culture. In this case, the utterance refers to an episode in an overseas tradition expedition of these natives, in which several canoes take part in a competitive spirit. This last-mentioned feature explains also the emotional nature of the utterance: it is not a mere statement of fact, but a boast, a piece of self-glorification, extremely characteristic of the Trobrianders' culture in general and of their ceremonial barter in particular.

▷ *Note down one or two utterances from a conversation you have overheard. Write down everything an outsider would need to know in order to understand the full meaning of these utterances in their situational and cultural context.*

Text 9

BRONISLAW MALINOWSKI: *Coral Gardens and their Magic.* Vol. II. Dover 1978, page 53.

Rites and rituals are a prime example of meaning as action. However, the power of the ritual does not reside in the words alone, but in the social structure that gives the person who utters them the legitimation, the authority, and the power to create and impose onto others a certain social reality.

There is no strict line of demarcation between the signature on a cheque, a civil contract of marriage, the sacramental vow on a similar occasion, the change of substance in the Holy Eucharist, and the repulsion of bush-pigs by means of a fictitious excrement. One of the contextual conditions for the sacred or legal power of words is the existence, within a certain culture, of beliefs, of moral attitudes and of legal sanctions.

What interests us in this type of speech is that, in all communities, certain words are accepted as potentially creative of acts. You utter a vow or you forge a signature and you may find yourself bound for life to a monastery, a woman or a prison. You utter another word and you make millions happy, as when the Holy Father blesses the faithful. Human beings will bank everything, risk their lives and substance, undertake a war or embark on a perilous expedition, because a few words have been uttered. The words may be the silly speech of a modern 'leader' or prime minister; or a sacramental formula, an indiscreet remark wounding 'national honour', or an ultimatum. But in each case words are equally powerful and fateful causes of action.

▷ Find other examples of the 'performative' function of certain words or phrases, i.e. where the mere utterance of a word performs the action intended.

▷ Show how the action is performed only if the context of situation is appropriate.

▷ In Text 8, Malinowski talks about the dependency of words on context. Here he talks about words being 'powerful and fateful causes of action.' Is there a contradiction here?

Text 10

CLIFFORD GEERTZ: *The Interpretation of Cultures.*
Basic Books 1973, pages 12, 13, 14.

In this chapter entitled 'Thick description: toward an interpretive theory of culture', Geertz lays the foundation for an anthropology that is both factually objective and interpretively subjective.

To play the violin it is necessary to possess certain habits, skills, knowledge, and talents, to be in the mood to play, and (as the old joke goes) to have a violin. But violin playing is neither the habits, skills, knowledge, and so on, nor the mood, nor (the notion believers in 'material culture' apparently embrace) the violin ... Culture is public because meaning is. You can't wink (or burlesque one) without knowing what counts as winking or how, physically, to contract your eyelids, and you can't conduct a sheep raid (or mimic one) without knowing what it is to steal a sheep and how practically to go about it. But to draw from such truths the conclusion that knowing how to wink is winking and knowing how to steal a sheep is sheep raiding is to betray as deep a confusion as, taking thin descriptions for thick, to identify winking with eyelid contractions or sheep raiding with chasing woolly animals out of pastures ... What, in places like Morocco, most prevents those of us who grew up winking other winks or attending other sheep from grasping what people are up to is not ignorance as to how cognition works ... [but] a lack of familiarity with the imaginative universe within which their acts are signs ...

Looked at in this way, the aim of anthropology is the enlargement of the universe of human discourse. This is not, of course, its only aim—instruction, amusement, practical counsel, moral advance, and the discovery of natural order in human behavior are others; nor is anthropology the only discipline which pursues it. But it is an aim to which a semiotic concept of culture is peculiarly well adapted. As interworked systems of construable signs (what, ignoring provincial usages, I would call symbols), culture is not a power, something to which social events, behaviors, institutions, or processes can be causally attributed; it is a context, something within which they can be intelligibly— that is, thickly—described.

▷ *What, according to Geertz, would an outsider have to understand in order to grasp the meaning of violin playing for a child raised in a musical family?*

▷ *Can you think of a phenomenon from your culture that outsiders cannot possibly understand if they don't understand 'the imaginative universe' within which this phenomenon is a sign?*

▷ *To what extent is Geertz' definition of culture similar to the one Malinowski illustrates in Text 8?*

Chapter 4
Spoken language, oral culture

Text 11
R. BROWN and A. GILMAN: 'The pronouns of power and solidarity' in Pier Paolo Giglioli (Ed.): *Language and Social Context*. Penguin 1972, pages 266, 269–70.

One of the major social deictic devices is the reciprocal or non-reciprocal use of personal pronouns and other forms of address. The reciprocal use of French 'tu' or 'vous' (German 'du' or 'Sie', Spanish 'tú' or 'usted') indicates symmetry in power relations among interlocutors. Non-reciprocal use of personal forms of address, such as when one speaker addresses the other with 'tu' but is addressed with 'vous', indicates a difference in power and status among interlocutors. The use of such forms varies historically and culturally.

A historical study of the pronouns of address reveals a set of semantic and social psychological correspondence. The non-reciprocal power semantic is associated with a relatively static society in which power is distributed by birthright and is not subject to much redistribution. The power semantic was closely tied with the feudal and manorial systems ... The static social structure was accompanied by the Church's teaching that each man had his properly appointed place and ought not to wish to rise above it. The reciprocal solidarity semantic has grown with social mobility and an equalitarian ideology ... In France the non-reciprocal power semantic was dominant until the Revolution when the Committee for the Public Safety condemned the use of V as a feudal remnant and ordered a universal reciprocal T... In England, before the Norman Conquest, 'ye' was the second person plural and 'thou' the singular. 'You' was originally the accusative of 'ye', but in time it also became the nominative plural and ultimately ousted 'thou' as the usual singular ...

We believe ... that the development of open societies with an equalitarian ideology acted against the non-reciprocal power semantic and in favor of solidarity. It is our suggestion that the larger social changes created a distaste for the face-to-face expression of differential power ... Award of the doctoral degree, for instance, transforms a student into a colleague and, among American academics, the familiar first name is normal. The fledgling academic may find it difficult to call his former teachers by their first names. Although these teachers may be young and affable, they have had a very real power over him for several years and it will feel presumptuous to deny this all at once with a new mode of address. However, the 'tyranny of democratic manners' does not allow him to continue comfortably with the polite 'Professor X'. He would not like to be thought unduly conscious of status, unprepared for faculty rank, a born lickspittle. Happily, English allows him a respite. He can avoid any term of address, staying with the uncommitted 'you', until he and his addressees have got used to the new state of things. The linguistic RITE DE PASSAGE has, for English speakers, a waiting room in which to screw up courage.

▷ *How do you think power differences are expressed in societies where there is no choice between second person pronoun forms (for example, 'tu'/'vous') in the language itself?*

▷ *In your view, how would 'an equalitarian ideology' affect the use of these pronouns, or other forms of address, in the languages you are familiar with?*

Text 12

ERVING GOFFMAN: 'Footing' in *Forms of Talk*.
University of Pennsylvania Press 1981, pages 124–5.

Power relations are expressed among speakers not only through social deictics but also through subtle changes in alignments of speaker to hearers, as the following example given by Goffman illustrates. The White House incident occurred during the small talk phase that usually follows more serious business, and that generally involves a change of tone and an alteration of the symmetrical power relationship between the President and representatives of the Press.

WASHINGTON [UPI]—President Nixon, a gentleman of the old school, teased a newspaper woman yesterday about wearing slacks to the White House and made it clear that he prefers dresses on women.

After a bill-signing ceremony in the Oval Office, the President stood up from his desk and in a teasing voice said to UPI's Helen Thomas: "Helen, are you still wearing slacks? Do you prefer them actually? Every time I see girls in slacks it reminds me of China."

Miss Thomas, somewhat abashed, told the President that Chinese women were moving toward Western dress.

"This is not said in an uncomplimentary way, but slacks can do something for some people and some it can't." He hastened to add, "but I think you do very well. Turn around."

As Nixon, Attorney General Elliott L. Richardson, FBI Director Clarence Kelley and other high-ranking law enforcement officials smiling [sic], Miss Thomas did a pirouette for the President. She was wearing white pants, a navy blue jersey shirt, long white beads and navy blue patent leather shoes with red trim.

Nixon asked Miss Thomas how her husband, Douglas Cornell, liked her wearing pants outfits.

"He doesn't mind," she replied.

"Do they cost less than gowns?"

"No," said Miss Thomas.

"Then change," commanded the President with a wide grin as other reporters and cameramen roared with laughter [*The Evening Bulletin* (Philadelphia), 1973]

This incident points to the power of the president to force an individual who is female from her occupational capacity into a sexual, domestic one during an occasion in which she ... might well be very concerned that she be given her full professional due, and that due only ... Behind this fact is something much more significant: the contemporary social definition that women must always be ready to receive comments on their "appearance", the chief constraints being that the remarks should be favorable, delivered by someone with whom they are acquainted, and not interpretable as sarcasm. Implied, structurally, is that a woman must ever be ready to change ground, or, rather, have the ground changed for her, by virtue of being subject to becoming momentarily an object of approving attention, not—or not merely—a participant in it.

▷ *In the incident as it is reported here, what do you think are the verbal and non-verbal aspects of the change of footing that Goffman talks about?*

▷ *This change in footing corresponds to a change in the frame that the President imposes on the events and that Helen Thomas is forced to accept. How would you characterize this change in frame?*

Text 13

PENELOPE BROWN and STEPHEN C. LEVINSON: *Politeness*. Cambridge University Press 1978, page 13.

The incident related in Text 12 illustrates the public facework that even a president has to do in order to put down a professional woman with impunity in a democratic society. Such facework is part of an elaborate system of politeness that has universal validity, even though its realization varies from culture to culture.

Cultural notions of 'face'

Central to our model is a highly abstract notion of 'face' which consists of two specific kinds of desires ('face-wants') attributed by interactants to one another: the desire to be unimpeded in one's actions (negative face), and the desire (in some respects) to be approved of (positive face). This is the bare bones of a notion of face which (we argue) is universal, but which in any particular society we would expect to be the subject of much cultural elaboration. On the one hand, this core concept is subject to cultural specifications of many sorts—what kinds of acts threaten face, what sorts of persons have special rights to face-protection, and what kinds of personal style (in terms of things like graciousness, ease of social relations, etc.) are especially appreciated .... On the other hand notions of face naturally link up to some of the most fundamental cultural ideas about the nature of the social persona, honour and virtue, shame and redemption and thus to religious concepts.

▷ *Analyze the incident related in Text 12 in terms of face. How does Nixon's behavior manage to both satisfy and threaten Helen Thomas' positive and negative face?*

▷ *Explain the differing reactions to personal compliments in France and in the US, mentioned on page 7, in terms of face-wants. Speculate as to how each links up to a different view of the social persona in France and in the US.*

Text 14

SHIRLEY BRICE HEATH: *Ways with Words.*
Cambridge University Press 1983, pages 186–187.

In her classical study of language, life, and work in three Black and White, working-class and middle-class, communities in the United States, Heath compares the 'ways with words' of adult residents of two communities only a few miles apart in the Piedmont Carolinas: 'Roadville', a white working-class community of families steeped for four generations in the life of the textile mills, and 'Trackton', a black working-class community whose older generations grew up farming the land, but whose current members work in the mills. Here she analyzes the narrative styles of adults in both communities.

In both communities, stories entertain; they provide fun, laughter, and frames for other speech events which provide a lesson or a witty display of verbal skill. In Roadville, a proverb, witty saying, or Scriptural quotation inserted into a story adds to both the entertainment value of the story and to its unifying role. Group knowledge of a proverb or saying, or approval of Scriptural quotation reinforces the communal experience which forms the basis of Roadville's stories. In Trackton, various types of language play, imitations of other community members or TV personalities, dramatic gestures and shifts of voice quality, and rhetorical questions and expressions of emotional evaluations add humor and draw out the interaction of story-teller and audience. Though both communities use their stories to entertain, Roadville adults see their stories as didactic: the purpose of a story is to make a point—a point about the conventions of behavior. Audience and story-teller are drawn together in a common bond through acceptance of the merits of the story's point for all. In Trackton, stories often have no point; they may go on as long as the audience enjoys the story-teller's entertainment. Thus a story-teller may intend on his first entry into a stream of discourse to tell only one story, but he may find the audience reception such that he can move from the first story into another, and yet another. Trackton audiences are unified by the story only in that they recognize the entertainment value of the story, and they approve stories which extol the virtues of an individual. Stories do not teach lessons about proper behavior; they tell of individuals who excel by outwitting the rules of conventional behavior.

▷ *How do you think these story-telling events illustrate the nature of spoken language (see Chapter 4)?*

▷ *What different kinds of 'truth' do you think are conveyed by these culturally different narrative styles?*

▷ *In Text 1, Sapir claims that the 'real world' is to a large extent built up on the 'language habits of the group'. Would it follow that the two groups of people described in this passage belong to two different cultures?*

Chapter 5
Print language, literate culture

Text 15
WALTER J. ONG: *Orality and Literacy*. Methuen 1982, pages 175, 178, 179.

The oral language can be seen as primary in that it develops naturally both in the life of the individual (ontogenetically) and in the history of humankind (phylogenetically); but writing, Ong argues, has forever changed the way human beings think and act in the world. Even people who don't know how to read or write are affected by modes of thought brought about by the technology of writing.

The interaction between the orality that all human beings are born into and the technology of writing, which no one is born into, touches the depths of the psyche. Ontogenetically and phylogenetically, it is the oral word that first illuminates consciousness with articulate language, that first divides subject and predicate and then relates them to one another, and that ties human beings to one another in society. Writing introduces division and alienation, but a higher unity as well. It intensifies the sense of self and fosters more conscious interaction between persons. Writing is consciousness-raising.

...

To say that a great many changes in the psyche and in culture connect with the passage from orality to writing is not to make writing (and/or its sequel, print) the sole cause of all the changes. The connection is not a matter of reductionism but of relationism. The shift from orality to writing intimately interrelates with more psychic and social developments than we have yet noted. Developments in food production, in trade, in political organ-ization, in religious institutions, in technological skills, in educational practices, in means of transportation, in family organization, and in other areas of human life all play their own distinctive roles. But most of these developments, and indeed very likely every one of them, have themselves been affected, often at great depth, by the shift from orality to literacy and beyond, as many of them have in turn affected this shift.

▷ *What does Walter Ong mean by the statement: 'Writing introduces division and alienation, but a higher unity as well'?*

▷ *Some scholars have pointed out that it is not writing* per se *that is 'consciousness-raising', especially under certain school conditions, but only certain uses of writing. Under what conditions can writing intensify a person's sense of self?*

Text 16

H.G. WIDDOWSON: 'The realization of rules in written discourse' in *Explorations in Applied Linguistics*. Oxford University Press 1984, page 39.

Literacy can intensify a sense of self only if written texts are put in relation with readers' selves, i.e. if they are read not just as linguistic products but as discourse.

Reading is most commonly characterized as an exercise in linguistic analysis, an activity whereby information is extracted from a written text which signals it. The information is thought to be *there*, statically residing in the text and in principle recoverable in its entirety. If, in practice, the reader cannot recover the information it is assumed that he is defective in linguistic competence. Such a view represents written language as the manifestation of syntactic and semantic rules and the reader's task as a matter of recognition. I want to propose an alternative view: one which represents written text as a set of directions for conducting an interaction. From such an interaction, which in effect creates discourse from text, the reader derives what information he needs, or what information his current state of knowledge enables him to take in. Meanings, in this view, are not contained in a text but are derived from the discourse that is created from it, and since this will be determined by such factors as limitation of knowledge and purpose in reading, these meanings can never be complete or precise. They are approximations. What I want to propose, then, is an approach to reading which focuses on the procedures which the language user employs in making sense of written communication.

▷ *Can you think of other factors that determine which discourse is created by readers from a text, besides 'limitation of knowledge and purpose in reading'?*

▷ *In Text 8, Malinowski demonstrates how 'linguistic data' alone cannot lead to an understanding of spoken language use. How far is this consistent with what Widdowson says here about written language?*

Text 17

JAMES GEE: *Social Linguistics and Literacies: Ideology in Discourses.* The Falmer Press 1990, pages 142–43.

Literacy, says Gee, is much more than just the ability to read and write. It is an ability to signal one's membership in a socially meaningful discourse community.

[A]t any moment we are using language, we must say or write the right thing in the right way while playing the right social role and (appearing) to hold the right values, beliefs and attitudes. What is important is not language, and surely not grammar, but *saying (writing)-doing-being-valuing-believing combinations.* These combinations I will refer to as 'Discourses' with a capital 'D' ('discourse' with a little 'd', I will use for connected stretches of language that make sense, like conversations, stories, reports, arguments, essays; 'discourse' is part of 'Discourse'—'Discourse' with a big 'D' is always more than just language). Discourses are ways of being in the world, or forms of life which integrate words, acts, values, beliefs, attitudes, social identities, as well as gestures, glances, body positions and clothes.

A Discourse is a sort of 'identity kit' which comes complete with the appropriate costume and instructions on how to act, talk, and often write, so as to take on a particular social role that others will recognize ...

Another way to look at Discourses is that they are always ways of displaying (through words, actions, values and beliefs) *membership* in a particular social group or social network (people who associate with each other around a common set of interests, goals and activities). Being 'trained' as a linguist meant that I learned to speak, think and act like a linguist, and to recognize others when they do so (not just that I learned lots of facts about language and linguistics). So 'being a linguist' is one of the Discourses I have mastered ... .

To sum up, by 'a Discourse' I mean:

A Discourse is a socially accepted association among ways of using language, of thinking, feeling, believing, valuing, and of acting that can be used to identify oneself as a member of a socially meaningful group or 'social network', or to signal (that one is playing) a socially meaningful 'role'.

▷ *How would you define 'a socially meaningful group'? Show through one or two examples not only that a Discourse is defined by the social group who uses it, but that it helps co-construct that social group as well (see Chapter 3).*

▷ *Can you think of a type of literacy that would enable someone precisely to subvert the Discourse of the group to which he/she belongs?*

Text 18

BILL COPE and MARY KALANTZIS (Eds.): *The Powers of Literacy. A Genre Approach to Teaching Writing.* University of Pittsburgh Press 1993, page 7.

To understand how Discourses operate in society, it is

important to understand the notion of 'genre'. It is through genres that texts are linked to their contexts of production and reception, i.e. to culture.

'Genre' is a term used in literacy pedagogy to connect the different forms text take with variations in social purpose. Texts are different because they do different things. So, any literacy pedagogy has to be concerned, not just with the formalities of how texts work, but also with the living social reality of texts-in-use ...

Genres are social processes. Texts are patterned in reasonably predictable ways according to patterns of social interaction in a particular culture. Social patterning and textual patterning meet as genres ... It follows that genres are not simply created by individuals in the moment of their utterance; to have meaning, they must be social. Individual speakers and writers act within a cultural context and with a knowledge of the different social effects of different types of oral and written text. Genres, moreover, give their users access to certain realms of social action and interaction, certain realms of social influence and power.

▷ *Compare this functional definition of 'genre' with the more traditional one you may find in the dictionary. What kind of link between language and culture is established by each of these definitions?*

▷ *Find one example of an oral and a written genre respectively that might give its users 'social influence and power'.*

▷ *How far is the notion of genre as discussed in this passage related to the notion of the literacy event as discussed on pages 60–1?*

Chapter 6
Language and cultural identity

Text 19
BENEDICT ANDERSON: *Imagined Communities.*
Verso 1983, pages 80, 81.

Print technology has played a major role in the development of a country's cultural identity because it fixes public memory of past events in a way that makes them understandable and hence memorable. These events can then be used by future generations to understand other events in that country's history.

Hobsbawm observes that 'The French Revolution was not made or led by a formed party or movement in the modern sense, nor by men attempting to carry out a systematic programme. It hardly even threw up "leaders" of the kind to which twentieth century revolutions have accustomed us, until the post-revolutionary figure of Napoléon.' But once it had occurred, it entered the accumulating memory of print. The overwhelming and bewildering concatenation of events experienced by its makers and its victims became a 'thing' – and with its own name: The French Revolution. Like a vast shapeless rock worn to a rounded boulder by countless drops of water, the experience was shaped by millions of printed words into a 'concept' on the printed page, and, in due course, into a model. Why 'it' broke out, what 'it' aimed for, why 'it' succeeded or failed, became subjects for endless polemics on the part of friends and foes: but of its 'it-ness', as it were, no one ever after had much doubt.

▷ *This author suggests that the concept of the French Revolution has been created through printed language. How far do you think this idea consistent with what is said in Text 6 about the conceptual power of metaphor?*

Text 20

R.B. LE PAGE and ANDRÉE TABOURET-KELLER: *Acts of Identity.* Cambridge University Press 1985, pages 13, 14.

Every act of language, be it written or spoken, is a statement about the position of its author within the social structure in a given culture. Through code-switchings and language crossings of all kinds, speakers signal who they are and how they want to be viewed at the moment of utterance.

[W]hatever views we may hold about the nature of linguistic systems and the 'rules' they embody, about 'correctness' in pronunciation, in grammar, in the meanings of words and so on—and most educated people do have views, sometimes very strong views, on these subjects—in our actual behaviour we are liable to be somewhat unpredictable .... The behaviour of the old lady telling the story in Belize provides us with a case in point. She began by using her most standard English; that was because she was talking directly to two visitors whom she knew were not Creole, and whom she assumed to be English. She started telling the story in what was more or less Creole English, and at a particular point where she related some crucial dialogue she switched into Spanish, finally reverting to Creole to finish the story off. Some of the characters of her story—for example, the carpenter, who evidently is a somewhat superior tradesman—speak in more standard English than others .... Here we introduce, then, the concept which is the theme of this book, that of linguistic behaviour as a series of *acts of identity* in which people reveal both their personal identity and their search for social roles.

▷ *In your opinion, why do educated people have such strong views about grammatical correctness if they themselves often speak 'incorrectly'?*

▷ *The authors here distinguish between personal identity and social roles. What do you think is the difference between them?*

Text 21
BEN RAMPTON: *Crossing: Language and Ethnicity among Adolescents.* Longman 1995, pages 280, 313.

While code-switching is usually seen as a device used to affirm a speaker's claim to solidarity with members who belong to two different language groups, crossing is seen as temporarily borrowing a language that is not your own. Rampton describes the language crossing practices of multiracial urban youth in British schools from among Panjabi, Caribbean Creole, and Stylized Asian English (SAE) language varieties.

Crossing ... focuses on code alternation by people who are not accepted members of the group associated with the second language they employ. It is concerned with switching into languages that are not generally thought to belong to you. This kind of switching, in which there is a distinct sense of movement across social or ethnic boundaries, raises issues of social legitimacy that participants need to negotiate, and that analysts could usefully devote more attention to. ...

[I]n Ashmead, crossing arose out of solidarities and allegiances that were grounded in a range of *non-ethnic* identities – identities of neighbourhood, class, gender, age, sexual orientation, role, recreational interest and so on – and it was these that generated, among other things, the local multiracial vernacular. It was their base in these connections that allowed adolescents to explore the significance of ethnicity and race through language crossing. Indeed, crossing not only emerged from a plurality of identity relations: it also addressed a range of the meanings that ethnicity could have. ...

Panjabi crossing was more independent of the ways in which ethnic minorities were generally represented than either Creole or SAE. In informal recreation, it took shape within the relatively subterranean traditions of playground culture, and in the context of bhangra [music] ... Crossing in Creole tended to reproduce popular conceptions and to accept and embrace its stereotypic connotations of vernacular vitality, counterposed to the values of bourgeois respectability ... With SAE, practical reinterpretation of established ideology took its most complex form. With white adults, crossing into Asian English evoked racist images of Asian deference in a manner that could subvert the action of any interlocutor that entertained them. Of course this could be done playfully, but at the moment when it was performed, crossing of this kind constituted an act of minor resistance to the smooth flow of adult-dominated interaction.

▷ *When an Anglo adolescent addresses a Bangladeshi fellow student with the Stylized Asian English (SAE) typical of Indian immigrants, what kind of 'social legitimacy' do you think needs to be negotiated?*

▷ *What factors, according to Rampton, allowed these adolescents to dare cross into languages that belonged to someone else and that they themselves didn't even fully master?*

▷ *Rampton's study shows how multiracial youth groups create for themselves a counter-culture through complex language crossings. What would you suppose are the characteristics of this counter-culture?*

Text 22

ALASTAIR PENNYCOOK: *The Cultural Politics of English as an International Language.* Longman 1994, pages 12, 13.

The spread of English around the world has usually been assumed to be natural, neutral, and beneficial. Pennycook puts in question all three assumptions, and argues that we have to see English as an international language in terms of the cultural identities it offers its speakers.

Sorely lacking from the predominant paradigm of investigation into English as an international language is a broad range of social, historical, cultural and political relationships. First, there is a failure to problematize the notion of choice, and therefore an assumption that individuals and countries are somehow free of economic, political and ideological constraints when they apparently freely opt for English. It is this failure to look critically at global relations that allows for a belief in the natural spread of English. Second, there is a structuralist and positivist view of language that suggests that all languages can be free of cultural and political influences; and, more particularly, there is a belief that by its international status English is even more neutral than other languages. And finally, there is an understanding of international relations that suggests that people and nations are free to deal with each other on an equal basis and thus, if English is widely used, this can only be beneficial ...

[A] number of writers have pointed to a far broader range of cultural and political effects of the spread of English: its widespread use threatens other languages; it has become the language of power and prestige in many countries, thus acting as a crucial gatekeeper to social and economic progress; its use in particular domains, especially professional, may exacerbate different power relationships and may render these domains more inaccessible to many people; its position in the world gives it a role also as an international gatekeeper, regulating the international flow of people; it is closely linked to national and increasingly non-national forms of culture and knowledge that are dominant in the world; and it is also bound up with aspects of global relations, such as the spread of capitalism, development aid and the dominance particularly of North American media.

▷ *Give examples to show that the spread of English as an international language is both an instrument of linguistic imperialism and a means for individual and societal empowerment.*

▷ *How do you think Pennycook's argument here supports the idea that language and culture are inevitably bound up with each other?*

▷ *In reference to Text 20, to what extent, in your view, can English as an international language serve to perform acts of identity?*

Chapter 7
Current issues

Text 23

BRAJ B. KACHRU: 'The alchemy of English. Social and functional power of non-native varieties' in Cheris Kramarae, Muriel Schulz, and William M. O'Barr (Eds.): *Language and Power.* Sage 1984, pages 190, 191.

The large-scale migrations of the last decades, and the spread of English around the world, have led linguists to question the notion of 'native speaker' and the monolingual native speaker norm in language use.

Since [Indian] independence, the controversy about English has taken new forms. Its "alien" power base is less an issue; so is its Englishness or Americanness in a cultural sense. The English language is not perceived as necessarily imparting only Western traditions. The medium is non-native, but the message is not. In several Asian and African countries, English now has national and international functions that are both distinct and complementary. English has thus acquired a new power base and a new elitism. The domains of English have been restructured. The result is that one more frequently, and very eloquently, hears people ask, 'Is English really a non-native ("alien") language for India, for Africa, and for Southeast Asia?' ...

The wider implications of this change in the ecology of world Englishes are significant: The new nativized (non-native) varieties have acquired an ontological status and developed localized norms and standards. Purists find that the situation is getting out of hand ... they are uncomfortable that the native speakers' norms are not universally accepted. There are others who feel that a pragmatic approach is warranted and that a 'monomodel' approach for English in the world context is neither applicable nor realistic.

▷ *Does the fact that English is used in many different cultural contexts mean, in your view, that the English language is a culturally neutral language?*

▷ *Do you think that the example of English as an international language confirms or invalidates the principle of linguistic relativity as described by Whorf in Text 2?*

Text 24

CHARLES TAYLOR: *Multiculturalism*. Edited by Amy Gutmann. Princeton University Press 1994, pages 37 and 38, 72 and 73.

In pre-modern times, people did not speak of 'identity' and 'recognition' because these were unproblematic, fixed as they were by one's social position in a hierarchical society. Modern societies that emphasize the equal dignity of all citizens make it difficult to recognize the unique cultural identity of an individual, because identities in modern societies are supposed to be formed in open dialogue, unshaped by a predefined social script. Thus the politics of democratic universalism clash with the politics of cultural difference.

With the move from honor to dignity has come a politics of universalism, emphasizing the equal dignity of all citizens, and the content of this politics has been the equalization of rights and entitlements ... With the politics of equal dignity, what is established is meant to be universally the same, an identical basket of rights and immunities; with the politics of difference, what we are asked to recognize is the unique identity of this individual or group, their distinctness from everyone else. The idea is that it is precisely this distinctness that has been ignored, glossed over, assimilated to a dominant or majority identity. ... There must be something midway between the inauthentic and homogenizing demand for recognition of equal worth, on the one hand, and the self-immurement within ethnocentric standards, on the other. There are other cultures, and we have to live together more and more, both on a world scale and commingled in each individual society.

What there is is the presumption of equal worth: a stance we take in embarking on the study of the other. Perhaps we don't need to ask whether it's something that others can demand from us as a right. We might simply ask whether this is the way we ought to approach others.

Well is it? How can this presumption be grounded? One ground that has been proposed is a religious one. Herder, for instance, had a view of divine providence, according to which all this variety of culture was not a mere accident but was meant to bring about a greater harmony. ... There is perhaps after all a moral issue here. We only need a sense of our own limited part in the whole human story to accept the presumption. It is only arrogance, or some analogous moral failing, that can deprive us of this. But what the presumption requires of us is not peremptory and inauthentic judgments of equal value, but a willingness to be open to comparative cultural study of the kind that must displace our horizons in the resulting fusions.

▷ *What do you think the author means by 'self-immurement within ethnocentric standards'? How is this opposed to the universalism based on a principle of universal equality?*

▷ *Can you find in your experience a time when your cultural horizon of understanding was 'displaced' as you entered into contact with a person from a different culture?*

SECTION 3
References

The references which follow can be classified into introductory level (marked ■□□), more advanced and consequently more technical (marked ■■□), and specialized, very demanding (marked ■■■).

Chapter 1
The relationship of language and culture

■■□

JOHN J. GUMPERZ and STEPHEN C. LEVINSON (Eds.): *Rethinking Linguistic Relativity*. Cambridge University Press 1996 (see Text 4).

This collection of papers re-examines ideas about linguistic relativity in the light of new evidence, and developments in anthropology, linguistics, and cognitive science.

■□□

WILHELM VON HUMBOLDT: *On Language: the diversity of human language-structure and its influence on the mental development of mankind.* (Tr. Peter Heath). Cambridge University Press 1988 [1836].

These philosophical considerations on the spirit of nations as expressed through their national languages have had an enormous influence on linguists and philosophers alike, especially in Europe and in the Soviet Union.

■■□

GEORGE LAKOFF: *Women, Fire, and Dangerous Things.
What Categories Reveal about the Mind*. University of
Chicago Press 1987.

This book deals with the relationship between language and
thought, and with the categories with which we apprehend
reality. Chapter 18 gives a fresh look at Whorf and relativism.

■□□

EDWARD SAID: *Orientalism*. Vintage 1979.

A provocative study of the colonialist representation of the Orient
by Western writers, i.e. their creation of an orientalist discourse
that has shaped both European and Middle-Eastern cultures to
this day.

■□□

EDWARD SAPIR: *Selected Writings of Edward Sapir in
Language, Culture, and Personality*. Edited by David G.
Mandelbaum. University of California Press 1949 (*see*
Texts 1 and 5).

A classic on language as a cultural and social product and on the
interplay of culture and personality. The essays on 'Language',
and 'The status of linguistics as a science' are particularly relevant
here.

■■□

EMILY A. SCHULTZ: *Dialogue at the Margins. Whorf,
Bakhtin and Linguistic Relativity*. University of Wisconsin
Press 1990.

This book looks at linguistic relativity by relating Whorfian
notions to the ideas of Bakhtin about dialogic interaction and its
variation within and across languages, and offers a new dialogic
interpretation of linguistic relativity.

■□□

BENJAMIN LEE WHORF: *Language, Thought and Reality:
Selected Writings of Benjamin Lee Whorf*. Edited by John B.
Carroll. M.I.T. Press 1956 (*see* Text 2).

This book is the classic foundation of the principle of linguistic relativity.

Chapter 2
Meaning as Sign

■■■

MICHEL FOUCAULT: *The Order of Things [Les Mots et les choses]*. Random House 1970.

This is an important, but challenging book, that discusses in an historical perspective how language has shaped the nature of knowledge and how cultural reality has been discursively constructed throughout the ages.

■■□

ROMAN JAKOBSON: 'Quest for the Essence of Language' in *Diogenes* 51, 1965.

In this often cited paper, Jakobson draws on Charles S. Peirce's semiotic philosophy to examine the non-arbitrary nature of some linguistic encodings in various languages.

■□□

GEORGE LAKOFF and MARK JOHNSON: *Metaphors We Live By*. University of Chicago Press, 1980 (*see* Text 6).

This extremely accessible book argues that metaphors are a part of everyday speech that affects the ways in which we perceive, think, and act. Reality itself is defined by metaphor, and as metaphors vary from culture to culture, so do the realities they define.

■□□

C. K. OGDEN and I. A. RICHARDS: *The Meaning of Meaning*. Harcourt, Brace and World 1923.

This book explores the influence of language on thought through a theory of signs. It includes a well-known supplementary essay by B. Malinowski on 'The problem of meaning in primitive languages' (*see* Text 8).

■■□

V. N. VOLOSINOV: *Marxism and the Philosophy of Language*. (Tr. L. Matejka and I.R. Titunik). Seminar Press 1973 [1929].

This important book deals with language as a system of signs, and with the laws that govern systems of signs within human society and culture. It offers a coherent philosophy for conceiving of the relationship of language, ideology, and human interaction.

■□□

ANNA WIERZBICKA: *Semantics, Culture, and Cognition*. Oxford University Press 1992 (*see* Text 7).

This book, written in simple, non-technical language, contains a wealth of examples to show that the lexicons of different languages suggest different conceptual universes and culture-specific meanings.

Chapter 3
Meaning as action

■■□

ERNST CASSIRER: *Language and Myth*. (Tr. Susanne Langer). Dover 1945.

This is an intellectually stimulating classic, that explores the place of language and myth in the pattern of human culture, the nature of word magic, and the relationship of culture and religion.

■■□

CLIFFORD GEERTZ: *The Interpretation of Cultures*. Basic Books 1973 (*see* Text 10).

This collection of essays on culture as a symbolic system is a must. Particularly important are Chapters 1 on thick description, 4 and 8 on religion and ideology as cultural systems, and the last chapter, 'Deep play: Notes on the Balinese cockfight'.

■■□

JOHN J. GUMPERZ: *Discourse Strategies*. Cambridge
University Press 1982.

This book develops a theory of conversational inference which
shows how individuals of different social and ethnic backgrounds
communicate with one another.

■■■

WILLIAM F. HANKS: *Language and Communicative
Practices*. Westview Press 1996.

This book offers new insights into the dynamics of context, the
indeterminacy of cultural forms, and the relation between human
experience and the making of meaning. Chapters 2 and 3 deal
with signs and meanings, Chapter 8 with linguistic relativity and
mediation.

■■□

BRONISLAW MALINOWSKI: *Coral Gardens and Their
Magic*. Dover 1978 [American Book Company 1935] (*see*
Texts 8 and 9).

Volume II contains an eminently readable ethnographic theory of
language based on the anthropologist's observations of the
Trobriand Islanders in the South Pacific.

Chapter 4
Spoken language, oral culture

■■■

PENELOPE BROWN and STEPHEN C. LEVINSON: *Politeness*.
Cambridge University Press 1978 (*see* Text 13).

This influential but rather technical book describes how different
cultures achieve the facework necessary to sustain polite behavi-
or, and proposes a model of politeness for analyzing the quality of
social relations in any society.

■■□

ERVING GOFFMAN: *Forms of Talk*. University of
Pennsylvania Press 1981 (*see* Text 12).

Of all of Goffman's books, this is the one that makes most explicit
the link between talk and the total physical, social, cultural, and
verbal environment in which it occurs.

■□□

DEBORAH TANNEN: *Conversational Style*. Ablex 1984.

A well-known analysis of talk at a Thanksgiving dinner among
friends from different US-American cultures.

■■□

DEBORAH TANNEN (Ed.): *Spoken and Written Language.
Exploring Orality and Literacy*. Vol. IX in the Series
'Advances in Discourse Processes', edited by Roy O. Freedle.
Ablex 1982.

This collection of papers examines oral and literate traditions in
various cultures and in various discourse genres.

■□□

SHIRLEY BRICE HEATH: *Ways with Words*. Cambridge
University Press 1983 (*see* Text 14).

A stimulating and accessible study of children learning to use
language at home and school in three communities in the United
States: 'Roadville', a White working-class community, 'Trackton', a Black working-class community, and 'Maintown', the
mainstream Black and White townspeople who hold power in the
schools and workplaces of the region.

Chapter 5
Print Language, Literate Culture

■■□

BENEDICT ANDERSON: *Imagined Communities*. Verso
1983 (*see* Text 19)

This influential book explores the interaction of capitalism,
nationalism, and print, and the development of vernacular
languages of nation-states.

■■■

NORMAN FAIRCLOUGH: *Discourse and Social Change.*
Polity Press 1992.

This book, representative of Critical Discourse Analysis, brings together text analysis, the analysis of processes of text production and interpretation, and the social analysis of discourse events.

■□□

JAMES GEE: *Social Linguistics and Literacies.* Falmer Press 1996 (see Text 17).

This book offers an interdisciplinary approach to the analysis of literacy, discourse, and language in educational settings with special reference to cross-cultural diversity.

■□□

WALTER J. ONG: *Orality and Literacy.* Methuen 1982 (*see* Text 15).

This classic explores some of the changes in our thought processes, personality, and social structures which, the author claims, are the result of the development of speech, writing, and print.

■■□

BRIAN V. STREET (Ed.): *Cross-Cultural Approaches to Literacy.* Cambridge University Press 1993.

The papers in this book investigate the meanings and uses of literacy in different cultures and societies.

■■□

JOHN M. SWALES: *Genre Analysis.* Cambridge University Press 1990.

Parts I and II define key concepts of genre and discourse community.

■■□

GEOFFREY WILLIAMS and RUQAIYA HASAN: *Literacy in Society.* Longman 1996.

This collection of articles takes a critical sociocultural approach to literacy and addresses issues of power, ideology, and politics associated with the technology of writing.

Chapter 6
Language and Cultural Identity

■■□

GLORIA ANZALDUA: *Borderland/La Frontera: The New Mestiza*. Spinsters/Aunt Lute 1987.

This book offers the feminist perspective of women of color on the construction of cultural difference through writing.

■■■

HOMI K. BHABHA: *The Location of Culture*. Routledge 1994.

In a series of interdisciplinary essays, the author redefines culture within a discourse framework and from a postcolonial perspective.

■■□

MICHEL DE CERTEAU: *The Practice of Everyday Life*. University of California Press 1984.

This interdisciplinary book looks at the way ordinary language can subvert the traditional meaning-making order of dominant cultures.

■■□

JAMES CLIFFORD and GEORGE E. MARCUS (Eds): *Writing Culture*. University of California Press 1986.

These important essays, drawing from historical, literary, anthropological, political, and philosophical sources, examine the problems created by the representation of culture through writing.

■■□

BRAJ B. KACHRU (Ed.): *The Other Tongue. English across Cultures* (2nd edn.) University of Illinois Press 1992.

This collection of papers examines the spread of English around the world from the point of view of linguistic variation. It deals with issues of intelligibility, nativization, contact and change, and suggests a pedagogy of 'World Englishes'.

■□□
ROBIN TOLMACH LAKOFF: *Talking Power*.
Basic Books 1990.

This book examines the politics of language and the way in which talk shapes and perpetuates power relationships within and across cultures, and gender cultures in particular.

■■□
R.B. LE PAGE and ANDRÉE TABOURET-KELLER: *Acts of Identity*. Cambridge University Press 1985 (see Text 20).

This extremely richly documented book uses language variation in West-Indian communities and in Britain to examine how language use plays out ethnic and other cultural identities.

■□□
ALASTAIR PENNYCOOK:*The Cultural Politics of English as an International Language*. Longman 1994 (*see* Text 22).

This book examines the spread of English around the world from the point of view of colonial and post-colonial, global politics. It deals with issues of power, nationalism and disciplinary politics, and suggests a critical pedagogy for teaching English as a 'worldly' language.

Chapter 7
Current issues

■□□
CLAIRE KRAMSCH: *Context and Culture in Language Teaching*. Oxford University Press 1993.

Drawing on insights from discourse analysis and cultural studies, this book represents an attempt to reconceptualize the study of spoken and written language as cultural study. It suggests a pedagogy of the intersubjective, intertextual, and intercultural in language teaching.

■□□

RON SCOLLON and SUZANNE WONG SCOLLON:
Intercultural Communication – A Discourse Approach.
Blackwell 1995.

This book focuses on the discourse of Asians and Westerners, of men and women, of corporate executives and professionals, and the discourse bridging generational cultures.

■■■

CHARLES TAYLOR: *Multiculturalism* (Ed. and introduced by Amy Gutmann). Princeton University Press 1994 (*see* Text 24).

In this sophisticated book, an initial essay by Charles Taylor on the **politics of recognition** is commented upon, and responded to, by several scholars including Jürgen Habermas and Anthony Appiah.

■■□

DENNIS TEDLOCK and BRUCE MANNHEIM (Eds): *The Dialogic Emergence of Culture.* University of Illinois Press 1995.

This collection of papers by anthropologists reformulate the idea of culture as continuously created and re-created in dialogs.

SECTION 4
Glossary

acculturation The process of internalizing the **culture** of a **discourse community**. *See* **socialization**. [6]

act of identity Way in which speakers display their cultural stance toward their membership in a specific **culture(2)**, and toward the culture of others through their use of language. [70]

appropriateness Characteristic of linguistic and social practices that meet the expectations of **native speakers** within their given culture; cf. **appropriation**. [80]

appropriation Process by which members of one **discourse community** make the language and the culture of another their own. [81]

arbitrariness The random nature of the fit between a linguistic **sign** and the object that it refers to, for example, the word 'rose' does not look like a rose. [16]

asymmetricality The lack of a perfect fit between a sign and its referent, between signifier and signified, for example, the sign 'rose' always means more than a flower of a certain shape and smell. [16]

barbarism Violation of the **standard language** by not fully competent speakers of the language (from Greek *barbaros*: outsider) [75]

code Formal system of communication. [3, 17]

code-switching Verbal strategy by which bilingual or bidialectal speakers change linguistic code within the same speech event as a sign of cultural solidarity or distance, and as an **act of** (cultural) **identity**. *See* **language crossing**. [43]

coherence The meaning created in the minds of speakers/readers by the **situated inferences** they make based on the words they hear/read; cf. **cohesion**. [28]

cohesion The semantic ties between units of language in a text; cf. **coherence**. [19]

cohesive device Linguistic element like a pronoun, demonstrative, conjunction, that encodes semantic continuity across a stretch of text. [19]

connotation The associations evoked by a word in the mind of the hearer/reader; cf. **denotation**. *See* **semantic networks**. [16, 23]

context of culture The historical knowledge, the beliefs, attitudes, values shared by members of a **discourse community**, and that contribute to the meaning of their verbal exchanges. [26]

context of situation The immediate physical, spatial, temporal, social environment in which verbal exchanges take place. [26]

context-dependent Characteristic of oral exchanges which depend very much for their meaning on the **context of situation** and the **context of culture** of the participants. [40]

context-reduced Characteristic of essay-type writing. Because readers are far removed in time and space from the author, the **text** itself must be able to make meaning without access to its original context of production; cf. **context-dependent**. [40]

contextualization cues A term coined by anthropologist John Gumperz to indicate the verbal, paraverbal and non-verbal signs that help speakers understand the full meaning of their interlocutors' utterances in context. [27]

conversational style A person's way of talking in the management of conversations. *See* **discourse accent**. [47]

co-operative principle A term coined by the philosopher Paul Grice to characterize the basic expectation that participants in informational exchanges will co-operate with one another by contributing appropriately and in a timely manner to the conversation. [31]

co-text The linguistic environment in which a word is used within a text. [19]

cultural identity Bureaucratically or self-ascribed membership in a specific **culture(2)**. [66]

cultural literacy Term coined by literary scholar E.D.Hirsch to refer to the body of knowledge that is presumably shared by all members of a given **culture**. [18]

culture 1 Membership in a **discourse community** that shares a common social space and history, and a common system of standards for perceiving, believing, evaluating, and acting. **2** The discourse community itself. **3** The system of standards itself. [4]

deictic Element of speech that points in a certain direction as viewed from the perspective of the speaker, for example, here, there, today, coming, going. *See* **deixis; index; social deixis**. [41]

deixis Process by which language indexes the physical, temporal, and social location of the speaker at the moment of utterance. *See* **index; social deixis**. [41]

denotation The basic conceptual meaning of a word. *See* **connotation**. [16, 23]

dialogic Based on dialog. [40]

diffusion Anthropological concept that refers to the process by which **stereotypes** are formed by extending the characteristic of one person or group of persons to all, for example, all Americans are individualists, all Chinese are collectivists. *See* **focusing**. [68]

Discourse This term, with a capital D, coined by linguist James Gee, refers, not only to ways of speaking, reading and writing, but also of behaving, interacting, thinking, valuing, that are characteristic of specific discourse communities. *See* **culture**. [61]

discourse The process of language use, whether it be spoken, written or printed, that includes writers, **texts**, and readers within a **sociocultural context** of meaning production and reception; cf. **text**. [57]

discourse accent A speaking or writing style that bears the mark of a **discourse community**'s ways of using language. *See* **conversational style**. [7]

discourse community A social group that has a broadly agreed set of common public goals and purposes in its use of spoken and written language; cf. **speech community**. [6, 17]

encoding The translation of experience into a sign or code. [15]

face A person's social need to both belong to a group and be independent of that group. [46]

facework The social strategies required to protect people's **face**. [46]

focusing Anthropological concept referring to the process by which **stereotypes** are formed by selectively focusing on certain classificatory concepts prevalent within a certain **discourse community**, for example, individualism vs. collectivism. *See* **diffusion**. [67]

footing A term coined by sociologist Erving Goffman to denote the stance we take up to the others present in the way we manage the production or reception of utterances. [42]

frame Culturally determined behavioral prototype that enables us to interpret each other's instances of verbal and non-verbal behavior. *See* **schema; structures of expectation**. [27]

genre A socially-sanctioned type of communicative event, either spoken, like an interview, or printed, like a novel. [62]

Great Divide Theory advanced by humanist Eric Havelock according to which the invention of writing created an irreducible difference between **oral** and **literate** cultures, and their ways of thinking. [56]

hegemony A term coined by Antonio Gramsci to refer to the predominant organizational form of power and domination across the economic, political, cultural and ideological domains of a society, or across societies. [9]

iconic A meaning of words based on resemblance of words to reality, for example, onomatopoeia ('bash', 'mash', 'smash', 'crash', 'dash'). [16, 23]

index 1 To index is to point to the presence of some entity in the immediate situation at hand. **2** An index is a linguistic form that performs this function. *See* **deictic**. [41]

intercultural 1 Refers to the meeting between people from different **cultures** and languages across the political boundaries of nation-states. **2** Refers to communication between people from different ethnic, social, gendered **cultures** within the boundaries of the same nation. *See* **multicultural**. [81]

language crossing The switch from one language code or variety to another, or stylization of one variety, or creation of hybrid varieties of the same code, as an **act of identity** or resistance. *See* **code-switching**. [70]

linguicism Term coined by Robert Phillipson to refer to discrimination and prejudice on the grounds of language, analogous to racism, sexism. [76]

linguistic imperialism Worldwide expansion of one language at the expense of others. [76]

linguistic nationism Association of one language variety (standard or national language) with membership of one national community. [72]

linguistic relativity principle A hypothesis advanced by the linguists Edward Sapir and Benjamin Whorf, according to which different languages offer different ways of perceiving and expressing the world around us, thus leading their speakers to conceive of the world in different ways. [11]

linguistic rights A concept promulgated by the UN and other international organizations to defend the right of peoples to develop and promote their own languages, in particular the right of children to have access to education in their languages; cf. **linguistic imperialism**. [76]

literacy The cognitive and sociocultural ability to use the written or print medium according to the norms of interaction and interpretation of a given discourse community. [37]

literacy event Interaction of a reader or community of readers with a written **text**. *See* **discourse**. [60]

literate Characteristic of the use of written language. *See* **literacy**. [37]

metaphor Not only a device of the poetic imagination and the rhetorical flourish, metaphor is a property of our conceptual system, a way of using language that structures how we perceive things, how we think, and what we do. [20]

multicultural Political term used to characterize a society composed of people from different cultures or an individual who belongs to several cultures. *See* **intercultural(2)**. [82]

narrative style A person's way of telling stories that reflects the uses of language of the **discourse community** he/she has been **socialized** into. *See* **conversational style; discourse accent**. [50]

native speaker A person who is recognized, linguistically and culturally, by members of a **discourse community** as being one of them. [79]

orality Features of **discourse** associated with the use of spoken language; cf. **literacy**. [37]

orate Characteristic of either spoken or written language that bears traces of **orality**; cf. **literate**. [37]

orientalism Term coined by Edward Said to denote the colonialist perspective taken by European writers on the Orient, and by extension, a colonialist view of any foreign culture. [9]

people-centered Characteristic of conversational exchanges where participants have to engage their listeners, not just convey information; cf. **topic-centered**. [39]

phatic communion Term coined by anthropologist Bronislaw Malinowski to characterize the ready-made chunks of speech like 'Hi, how are you?' that people use more to maintain social contact than to convey information. [38]

politics of recognition The political debates surrounding the right of minorities to be legitimately recognized and accepted as members of a **culture(2)** that is different from the dominant culture. *See* **legitimation**. [79, 124]

pragmatics The study of what speakers mean with words, as distinct from what the **code** means. [15]

print culture The artifacts, mindsets, and social practices associated with the production and reception of printed language; cf. **orality; literacy**. [54]

prior text One or several texts which a given text explicitly cites, refers to, or builds upon, or which it implicitly harks back to, evokes, or in some way incorporates. [19, 61]

referent Object that a signifier (sound or word) points to, for example, a flower of a certain shape and smell is the referent for the word 'rose'. [16]

representation The way a **culture(2)** expresses itself, or is expressed by others, through linguistic, visual, artistic, and non-artistic means. [9]

Sapir-Whorf hypothesis The **linguistic relativity** hypothesis advanced by linguists Edward Sapir and Benjamin Whorf. *See* **linguistic relativity principle.** [11]

schema (plural **schemata**) Mental representation of typical instance used in discourse processing to predict and make sense of the particular instance which the discourse describes. *See* **structures of expectation; frame.** [27]

semantic networks Associations of related meanings evoked by words. [17]

semantics The study of how meaning is encoded in language, as distinct from what speakers mean to say when they use language. [15]

sign The relation between a signifier (word or sound) and the signified (image or concept). [3, 15]

situated inferences Mental links made by participants in verbal exchanges between the words spoken and the relevant **context of situation** and **context of culture.** [27]

social deixis Process by which language **indexes(1)** not only the physical and temporal location of the speaker at the moment of speaking, but also his/her social status and the status given to the addressee. *See* **deixis.** [41]

socialization The process by which a person internalizes the conventions of behavior imposed by a society or social group. *See* **acculturation.** [6]

sociocultural context The synchronic (social, societal) and the diachronic (historical) context of language use, also called sociohistorical context. [8]

speech community A social group that shares knowledge of one linguistic code and knowledge also of its patterns of use; cf. **discourse community.** [5, 17]

standard language Artificially conventionalized linguistic code, fashioned from a multiplicity of dialects spoken within a national community, and imposed as the national code. *See* **linguistic nationism.** [74]

stereotype Conventionalized ways of talking and thinking about other people and cultures. *See* **symbol.** [22]

structures of expectation Mental structures of knowledge that enable us to understand present events and anticipate future ones. *See* **frame; schema.** [27]

symbol Conventionalized sign that has been endowed with special meaning by the members of a given culture. [22]

technology of the word This phrase, coined by the humanist Walter Ong, refers to the written or print medium. [5]

text The product of language use, whether it be a conversational exchange, or a stretch of written prose, held together by **cohesive devices**; cf. **discourse.** [57]

topic-centered Characteristic of essay-type writing, where the transmission of a message is of prime importance; cf. **people-centered.** [39]

Acknowledgments

The author and publisher are grateful for the use of the following extracts and adaptations of copyright material:

Ablex Publishing Corporation for permission to reproduce an extract from *Conversational Style: Analyzing Talk Among Friends* by Deborah Tannen (1984), published by Ablex.

Addison Wesley Longman Ltd for permission to reproduce two extracts from *Crossing: Language and Ethnicity among Adolescents* by Ben Rampton (Longman, 1995); and an extract from *The Cultural Politics of English as an International Language* by Alastair Pennycook (Longman, 1994).

Cambridge University Press for permission to reproduce extracts from: 'Introduction: Linguistic relativity re-examined' by John J. Gumperz and Stephen C. Levinson, in J. Gumperz and S. Levinson (eds): *Rethinking Linguistic Relativity* (1996); *Politeness* by Penelope Brown and Stephen C. Levinson (1978); *Ways with Words* by Shirley Brice Heath (1983); from *Acts of Identity* by R. B. Le Page and Andrée Tabouret-Keller (1985); *Talking Voices: Repetition, Dialogue and Imagery in Conversational Discourse* by Deborah Tannen (1989); *Discourse Strategies* by John J. Gumperz (1982).

Center for Applied Lingusitics and the author for permission to reproduce an extract from *Discourse Analysis and Second Language Teaching* by Claire Kramsch.

Falmer Press for permission to reproduce an extract from *Social Linguistics and Literacies: Ideology in Discourses* by James Gee (1990); and an extract from Bill Cope and Mary Kalantzis (eds.): *The Powers of Literacy: A Genre Approach to Teaching Writing* (1993).

S. Fischer Verlag, Berlin for permission to reproduce an extract from *Der Zauberberg* by Thomas Mann, Copyright 1924.

HarperCollins Publishers, Inc. for an extract from *The Interpretation of Cultures* by Clifford Geertz (Basic Books, 1973)

MIT Press for permission to reproduce an extract from *Language, Thought and Reality: Selected Writings of Benjamin Lee Whorf* edited by John B. Carroll (MIT, 1956); and an extract from 'The Pronouns of power and solidarity' by R. Brown and A. Gilman, from Thomas A. Sebeok (ed.): *Style in Language* (MIT, 1964).

Wm Morrow & Co., Inc. for an extract from *The Language Instinct* by Steven Pinker.

National Centre for Industrial Language Training for extracts from *Cross-Talk. A Study of Cross Cultural Communication* by John J. Gumperz, T. C. Jupp, and Celia Roberts (1977).

Oxford University Press for permission to reproduce extracts from 'The realization of rules in written discourse' in *Explorations in Applied Linguistics* by H. G. Widdowson (1984); and *Spoken and Written Language* by M. A. K. Halliday (1985).

Oxford University Press, Inc. for permission to reproduce an extract from *Semantics, Culture, and Cognition* by Anna Wierzbicka (1992), and for extracts from 'Cultural differences in framing: American and Japanese group discussions' by Suwako Watanabe and 'What's in a frame?' by D. Tannen in D. Tannen (ed.): *Framing in Discourse* (1993).

Princeton University Press for permission to reproduce an extract from *Multiculturalism* by Charles Taylor. Copyright © 1994 by Princeton University Press.

Random House for permission to reproduce an extract from *The Magic Mountain* by Thomas Mann, published by Martin Secker & Warburg.

Routledge for permission to reproduce an extract from *Orality and Literacy* by Walter Ong (Methuen & Co, 1982); and an extract from 'The Problem of Meaning in Primitive Languages' by Bronislaw Malinowski in C. K. Ogden and I. A. Richards (eds.): *The Meaning of Meaning* (Routledge & Kegan Paul).

Sage Publications, Inc. for permission to reproduce an extract from 'The alchemy of English: social and functional power of non-native varieties' by Braj B. Kachru in Cheris Kramarae, Muriel Schulz, and William M O'Barr (eds.): *Language and Power* (1984).

University of California Press for permission to reproduce extracts from David G Mandelbaum (ed.): *The Selected Writings of Edward Sapir in Language, Culture, and Personality* Copyright © 1949 The Regents of the University of California.

University of Chicago Press for permission to reproduce an extract from *Metaphors We Live By* by George Lakoff and Mark Johnson (University of Chicago Press, 1980).

University of Pennsylvania Press: for permission to reproduce an extract from 'Footing' in *Forms of Talk* by Erving Goffman (1981), Copyright 1981 by Erving Goffman. Grateful acknowledgment is made to *Semiotica* where this paper first appeared (25 [1979]: 1- 29).

Verso for permission to reproduce an extract from *Imagined Communities* by Benedict Anderson (Verso, 1983).

Although every effort has been made to trace and contact copyright holders before publication, this has not been possible in some cases. We apologize for any apparent infringement of copyright and if notified, the publisher will be pleased to rectify any errors or omissions at the earliest opportunity.